A
GUIDE TO TRACING YOUR
DONEGAL ANCESTORS

Helen Meehan
and
Godfrey Duffy

D1333581

FLYLEAF PRESS

First published in 1995

Second edition 2008

Flyleaf Press
4 Spencer Villas
Glenageary
Co. Dublin, Ireland
www.flyleaf.ie

© 2008 Flyleaf Press

British Library cataloguing in Publications Data available

ISBN 978-0-9539974-9-7

The information in this book is subject to change without notice.

Cover Illustration by Cathy Henderson

Page layout by Brian Smith.

Printed by Colour Books

Dedications

Helen Meehan: *To my late father, Robert Montgomery.*

Godfrey Duffy: *To my late father, Frank, whose pride in his Clonmany roots was an inspiration to me.*

Acknowledgements

Helen Meehan wishes to thank the following for their valuable assistance:

- NAI – Gregory O'Connor and Rosaleen Underwood
- Manuscript Department of the NLI – Máire Ní Chonaillain
- Folklore Dept U.C.D. – Seamus Ó Cathain, Cristoir MacCarthaigh and Bairbre Ni Fhloinn.
- RIA - Siobhan Fitzpatrick.
- Ulster Historical Foundation, Belfast – William Roulston.
- PRONI – Heather Stanley
- Central Library, Belfast – Jim Rutherdale
- University of Limerick – Dr. Matthew Potter.
- Donegal County Library - Eileen Burgess and her staff, especially Bernie Campbell and Una Matthewson.
- Donegal Archives – Niamh Brennan and Ciara Joyce.
- Donegal Ancestry – Susan McCaffrey.
- Enniskillen Library – Marianna Maguire and Margaret Kane
- Omagh Library – Belinda Mahaffy.
- Cardinal O'Fiach Library, Armagh – Roddy Hegarty
- Central Library, Derry – Gerry Quinn and Jean Nioclas.

Also Sean Beattie, Editor of Donegal Annual; Committee members of the Donegal Historical Society; Margaret Graham, Laghey; Mick and Pauline Maule-Oatway, Ascot, U.K.; the Coane-Leibell family, Connecticut USA; Eunan O'Donnell, Ardara and King's Inns, Dublin and Aine Ní Dhuibhne of the Rathmullan and District History Society.

A special word of thanks to my family: Dr. Eucharia, Rosaire, Edward and Roberta and especially my husband John for their patience and encouragement.

Godfrey Duffy wishes to thank the following for their valuable assistance: The NAI; The NLI; New York Public Library; Donegal Ancestry; Buckinghamshire County Council Archives; PRONI; The National Archives (London); Sean Beattie, Editor of the Donegal Annual; Catherine McWilliams, Historian and Genealogist; and Marius O'hEarcain, Editor of "It's Us They're Talking About" and a founder member of the Clonmany Festival and McGlinchey Summer School.

Table of Contents

Abbreviations Used

BL	British Library
BMD	Births, marriages and deaths
c.	circa (around)
Co.	County
C of I	Church of Ireland
DAL	Donegal Ancestry Ltd. (see p. 149)
DCA	Donegal County Archives (see p. 149)
DCL	Donegal County Library
DHS	Donegal Historical Society (see p. 149)
Don. Ann.	Donegal Annual (see p. 149)
Ed.	Edited
GO	Genealogical Office
GRO	General Register Office
IED	Irish Emigration Database
IGRS	Irish Genealogical Research Society
IMC	Irish Manuscripts Commission
Inc.	including
JAPMD	Journal of Assoc for Preservation of Memorials of the Dead
KA	Kabristan Archives (See p. 68)
LC	Local Custody
LDS	Church of Jesus Christ of Latter Day Saints Family History Library
LHL	Linenhall Library
Ms(s)	manuscript(s)
NAI	National Archives of Ireland
n.d.	no date
NLI	National Library of Ireland
NS	National School
OS	Ordnance Survey
PLU	Poor Law Union
PRO	Public Record Office (Now part of National Archives)
PRONI	Public Record Office of Northern Ireland
pub.	published/publisher
RC	Roman Catholic
RCBL	Representative Church Body Library (see p. 147)
re	relating to
RIA	Royal Irish Academy (see p. 146)
UCD	University College Dublin. Archives see www.ucd.ie/archives/

Chapter 1 Introduction

Geographically in the North and politically in the South, Co. Donegal is situated in the North West corner of Ireland.

The county can be divided into four main regions – in the extreme north, between Lough Foyle and Lough Swilly, lies the Inishowen Peninsula, containing the Baronies of Inishowen East and West. To the south – between the Foyle, Finn and Swilly rivers lies the Laggan – the most fertile part of the county containing the Baronies of Raphoe North and South.

West and North of the Laggan are the Donegal Highlands – the most barren and least fertile part of the county containing the Baronies of Boylagh and Kilmacrennan. South of the Blue Stacks Mountains lies the Donegal Bay area – the most fertile part being the coastal area between Killybegs and Ballyshannon. It contains the Baronies of Banagh and Tyrhugh.

Traditionally Donegal depended largely on farming, fishing and associated industries. Tweed and other cottage industries also contributed considerably to the economy of the county. However, today the county hosts many overseas firms which give significant employment, as do the service industries.

The population of the county has fluctuated considerably over the past two centuries. It peaked in 1841 at 296,448, but by 1851, following the Great Famine, it had fallen to 255,158. The fall continued and by 1911 it was only 168,537. In 1926 after the establishment of the Free State the population was 152,508. It had fallen to its lowest by 1971 when the county population was down to 108,344. Since then the population has risen – it was 137,575 in 2002 and 147,264 in 2006. This 7% growth is somewhat slower than the 8.2% recorded nationwide for the same period.

History
Donegal was populated from Neolithic times but we have no written records before the introduction of Christianity in the 5th century.

Early in the 5th century three sons of Niall of the Nine Hostages, the Gaelic King of Tara, came to the North West, defeated the early inhabitants and carved out kingdoms for themselves. From West of the Swilly to West of Barnes became Conals land – known in Gaelic as Tír Chonaill, Inishowen Peninsula became Eoghan's land and the area known today as the Laggan became the land of Enna. Over the centuries the Cinel Connal or Conall's people, spread East and conquered the Cinel Enna and the Cinel Eoghan moved East across the Foyle and carved out the new territories for themselves – Tír Eoghan – Eoghan's land – which has been anglicized to Tyrone.

By the 13th century the O'Donnells had become the dominant sept in Tyrconnel and were the chiefs for the following four centuries. About the same time the O'Neills became the dominant clan of the Cinel Eoghan. The clans themselves consisted of many families bound together by blood ties which were strengthened by fosterage. Unlike England and other European counties where the primogeniture system of succession was the norm, according to Brehon Law in Ireland anybody within the deirbhfinne (three generations) was entitled to succeed as leader. This led to much warfare within the clans as well as with neighbouring chiefs over territorial disputes.

Neither the Viking (9th –10th centuries) nor the later Norman (1169) invasions had much impact on North West Ulster. The first attempt by Britain to exert control was by the Tudors. By the 1590s the three southerly Irish provinces of Munster, Leinster and Connacht were largely under English control. Ulster was still the most Gaelic of the Provinces – the Reformation of Henry VIII and the later 1560 Acts of Uniformity and Supremacy had no effect in Donegal. But the winds of change were blowing and the O'Donnell's found it expedient to be friendly with the English (they still retained Brehon Law, tanistry, etc.) and the county was nominally shired in 1585.

The greatest resistance to the English conquest of Ireland began in 1594 when the O'Neills and O'Donnells laid aside their age old rivalries and, with other northern chiefs, especially the Maguires, rose in arms to defend their lands and way of life. The Irish were depending on aid from Spain, then the great Catholic power on the continent. But Spanish help came too late and landed in the wrong place – Kinsale in Cork. The Ulster army hurried south but the ensuing debacle of Kinsale (1601) broke the power of the Northern Chiefs. The Treaty of Mellifont followed in March 1603 and for the first time all of Ireland was under control of the Crown. The Chiefs were pardoned and created Earls. But the Brehon Law tanistry and gavelkind were all to be abolished. The Earls, finding it difficult to adapt to the changes, and fearful of their lives, went to Spain to seek help. This event is known as the "Flight of the Earls" and took place on 14th September 1607.

Their lands were then declared forfeit to the Crown and were given to English and Scottish adventurers who undertook (hence the name undertakers) to each bring Scottish or English tenants and artisans to take over the land. Deserving or loyal natives were given land in part of the Barony of Kilmacrennan but they only had leases for their own lifetime and these lands had been lost by the end of the 17th century.

Plantation brought many newcomers to Donegal and other Ulster counties. However, Donegal was less attractive than the other counties to these settlers, due to the nature of much of the land, and was therefore relatively less affected by this plantation. Many of the tenant farmers who came were Presbyterian. Landlords and officials had to be members of the Established Church.

The 18th century is usually known as the Era of the Anglo-Irish Ascendancy and until the latter part of the century the Penal Laws against Catholics and Dissenters remained on the Statute Books. The Toleration Act of 1719 exempted the Dissenters from the worst of the penalties but by now they were emigrating in large numbers to the New World. The 19th century saw many changes take place – Catholic Emancipation in 1829 restored Catholics as citizens, the Great Famine of 1845-47 devastated the county and in 1869 the Church of Ireland was disestablished.

The Land War with its slogan "The Land of Ireland for the people of Ireland" began in the 1880s and finally bore fruit with a succession of Land Acts. Most of the land of Donegal was bought out by new landowners, mostly local people, under the Wyndham Act of 1903. After the War of Independence Donegal became part of the new Irish Free State, which later became the Republic of Ireland.

This guide concentrates on the Donegal records available for tracing the various families which have lived, and continue to live, in Donegal. It is the second edition of this guide and has been updated to include websites and online information useful to anyone researching Donegal ancestry.

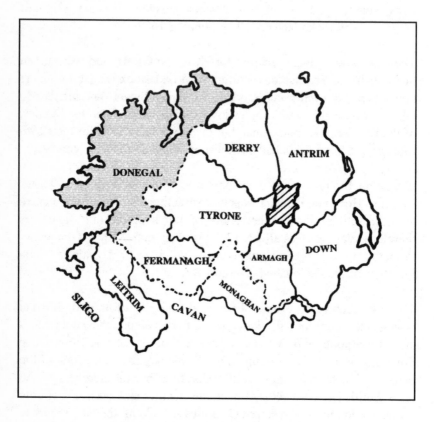

Donegal and its surrounding counties.
The border between Northern Ireland and the Republic of Ireland
is indicated by the dotted lines.

Chapter 2 How to Use this Book

The family name(s), and perhaps some oral tradition or documentary evidence, is often the only vestige of our ancestry. However, many people who are justly proud to claim Irish descent will want to investigate more fully their history and origins. By doing so, they can place their family in the context of the history of their country and county, and see them as real people who lived through, and perhaps significantly contributed to, great and traumatic times in Irish history. This book sets out to assist those with Donegal origins to learn about their ancestry. It is designed to guide the reader through the many types of documents and sources which record the lives of the people of Donegal.

The bulk of genealogical material relating to Donegal refers to the 19th century. Major sources include the Primary Valuation and Tithe Applotment Books which list people occupying land in the county (see Chap.6). The Land Records chapter, which includes estate papers, can provide information on ancestor's location from the 18th to 20th century (see Chap.9).

Parish registers are also a rich source of genealogical material and may be the only records of many Donegal people of the 18th and 19th centuries. The Church Records chapter provides information on the majority of extant parish registers with parish maps for Catholic and Church of Ireland parishes (see Chap. 6).

Civil registration for all Irish births, marriages and deaths began in 1864 and lists of Co. Donegal registration areas and records available are given in Chapter 7. National school registers are another useful source for locating ancestors once their parish is verified (see Chap.12). Pension claims are another source for locating ancestors (see p. 29).

Ancestors who belonged to more specific trade, military or social groups can be located in the census substitutes (see Chap. 5). By the close of the 19th century our more enterprising ancestors were using the newspapers and commercial directories to advertise their businesses (see Chaps. 10 and 11). It is always worth consulting Wills as a source of genealogical information, although the making of wills was dependent on religion and station in life (see Chap. 8). Finally Donegal family histories have been written on a professional and amateur basis. Some have been published and both originals and abstracts may be found in libraries and other institutions (see Chap. 13).

There are many starting points for your family history and a logical first point is by asking relations about family stories and known connections. In this context, elderly relations are generally helpful but a relation need not necessarily be elderly to be knowledgeable.

To organize your family history investigation of 'missing' and known family members, a 'Family Tree' chart should be drawn up using one of the current family tree packages installed on your PC. In both formats copies of the information should be held elsewhere in case one version of the information is accidentally destroyed.
In constructing your family history good preparation is important. To this end a few practical guidelines are suggested.

1. It is useful to know the basic history of Co. Donegal at a county and relevant parish level. This will allow you to understand local events which may have affected your family and have resulted in useful records.
2. Set a goal for your research, e.g. tracing a specific line of descent or finding a specific ancestor, rather than trying to trace all ancestral lines at the same time.
3. Record all the information you obtain, including conversations, with details of where and when it was found or recorded. It is in the nature of genealogy that the significance of material initially examined may not be realised until later.
4. Begin your research with yourself and proceed into the past one generation at a time, i.e. always work from the known to the unknown.

Chapter 3 Administrative Divisions
and Guides

An ancestor's address is an essential part of their identity. It is therefore important to understand the land divisions used, and the context in which an 'address' is cited. Most of the records useful in family research were drawn up by some national agency or local administration, whether of a governmental, religious or other nature. To find family information in these records, it is important to know the areas within which these administrators worked.

The following are the land divisions used in Co. Donegal. They are referred to extensively within the book, and a knowledge of them is important.

Province: The four provinces of Ireland, Connacht, Leinster, Munster and Ulster date from at least the 5th century. Co. Donegal is in the province of Ulster as are the counties Antrim, Armagh, Cavan, Derry, Down, Fermanagh, Monaghan and Tyrone. The term 'Ulster' is sometimes used incorrectly in some popular contexts to denote the six counties of Ireland, which are regarded as being within the UK. However, the Ulster counties of Donegal, Cavan and Monaghan are within the Republic of Ireland.

County: The division of Ireland into counties began in the late 12th century with Dublin and the process gradually continued until the formation of the last county, Wicklow in 1606. Co. Donegal was formed in 1585 and consolidated by the plantation of Ulster in the early 1600s. It is a major administrative unit for record purposes (see map p. 10).

1	Clonca	29	All Saints
2	Clonmany	18	Aughaninshin
3	Donagh	16	Aughnish (3 parts)
4	Culdaff (2 parts)	25	Burt
5	Moville Lower (2 parts)	10	Clonahorky
6	Moville Upper	1	Clonca
7	Clondavaddog	7	Clondavaddog
8	Tullaghobegley	35	Clonleigh
9	Raymunterdoney (4 parts)	2	Clonmany
10	Clonahorky	36	Convoy
11	Mevagh	17	Conwal
12	Tullyfern	4	Culdaff (2 parts)
13	Killygarvan	20	Desertegney
14	Garten	3	Donagh
15	Kilmacrennan (3 parts)	39	Donaghmore
16	Aughnish (3 parts)	48	Donegal
17	Conwal	49	Drumholm
18	Aghanunshin	21	Fahan Lower
19	Mintiaghs or Barr of Inch	22	Fahan Upper
20	Desertegney	14	Garten
21	Fahan Lower	42	Glencolmcille
22	Fahan Upper	24	Inch
23	Muff	28	Inishkeel
24	Inch	52	Innishmacsaint
25	Burt	46	Inver
26	Templecrone	51	Kilbarron
27	Lettermacward	43	Kilcar
28	Inishkeel	45	Killaghtee (2 parts)
29	All Saints	33	Killea
30	Leck (2 parts)	41	Killybegs Lower (2 parts)
31	Raymochy	44	Killybegs Upper
32	Taughboyne	13	Killygarvan
33	Killea	47	Killymard (2 parts)
34	Raphoe	15	Kilmacrennan (3 parts)
35	Clonleigh	37	Kilteevogue
36	Convoy	30	Leck (2 parts)
37	Kilteevogue	27	Lettermacward
38	Stranorlar	11	Mevagh
39	Donaghmore	19	Mintiaghs or Barr of Inch
40	Urney	5	Moville Lower (2 parts)
41	Killybegs Lower (2 parts)	6	Moville Upper
42	Glencolmcille	23	Muff
43	Kilcar	34	Raphoe
44	Killybegs Upper	31	Raymochy
45	Killaghtee (2 parts)	9	Raymunterdoney (4 parts)
46	Inver	38	Stranorlar
47	Killymard (2 parts)	32	Taughboyne
48	Donegal	50	Templecarn
49	Drumholm	26	Templecrone
50	Templecarn	8	Tullaghobegley
51	Kilbarron	12	Tullyfern
52	Innishmacsaint	40	Urney

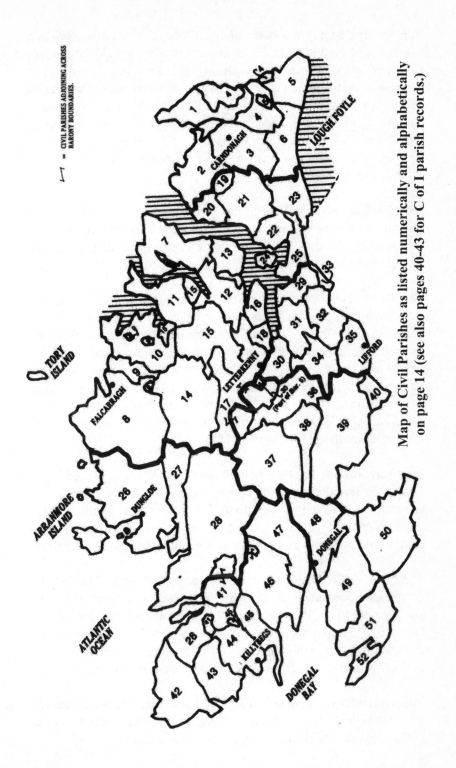

Map of Civil Parishes as listed numerically and alphabetically on page 14 (see also pages 40-43 for C of I parish records.)

Barony: The barony was based on the old Gaelic division known as a "Tuath". The barony is used in the Books of Survey and Distribution, Civil Survey and Down Survey. During the 18th century county rates were fixed by the Grand Jury and paid on a barony basis. Once again in the 19th century the barony was used in Griffith's Valuation. Its use continued into the 20th century when it was used as an enumeration unit in the 1901 census. The baronies of Co. Donegal are Banagh, Boylagh, East and West Inishowen, Kilmacrenan, North and South Raphoe and Tirhugh.

Civil Parish: This is perhaps the most widely used land division in local records. A civil parish may encompass several unconnected pieces of land in a single county, and may straddle a county boundary. In general civil parishes coincide with the Church of Ireland parishes.

Townland: This is the smallest of the administrative divisions, with size varying from a few acres to over 7,000 acres. In rural areas the townland is the basic 'address' used by people. Generations of the same family lived within certain townlands, to the extent that local people will associate a particular family with a townland and vice versa. A complete list of the townlands of Ireland and their location (within barony, civil parish, PLU etc) can be found in the 'General Alphabetical Index to the Townlands and Towns, Parishes and Baronies of Ireland' published by Thoms in 1861.

Poor Law Union: The Poor Law Union Relief Act of 1838 established a tax to be levied on property owners for the welfare of the poor. For this purpose the country was divided into Poor Law Unions (PLU). Each union had a workhouse based in a major town and the PLUs were named after these towns. For information on the records see page 134.

The PLUs of Co. Donegal were Ballyshannon, Donegal, Dunfanaghy, Glenties, Inishowen (in Carndonagh), Letterkenny, Londonderry, Milford and Stranorlar. The PLUs of Derry and Strabane covered part of East Donegal. This administrative unit was later used for other purposes such as civil registration, and elections. For the latter purpose, each union was further sub-divided into District Electoral Divisions.

Superintendent Registrar's Districts: These areas are geographically identical to the PLUs (see above) and were used as administrative areas in the collection of births, marriages and deaths records.

Ecclesiastical Divisions

The churches had their own systems of administration, although there are some correlations. The Synod of Kells in 1152 established the archdioceses of Armagh, Cashel, Dublin and Tuam. The Armagh archdiocese contains the dioceses of Derry, Clogher and Raphoe and parts of each encompass Co. Donegal. Their diocesan centres are at Derry, Monaghan and Letterkenny. Both Clogher and Raphoe have diocesan archives.

The Treaty of Mellifont (1603) brought all Ireland including Donegal, under control of the Crown for the first time. In 1605 the Act of Uniformity was proclaimed and the Church of Ireland became the State or Established Church and had legal responsibility for will probate, administration of marriages and other functions for all the people of Ireland. In effect, therefore the Church of Ireland was the civil power and its administrative units, particularly the parish, are both civil and ecclesiastical divisions. The Catholic Church, on the other hand, had no civil role or legal recognition. After 1699 the Catholic Church was effectively banned by the Penal Laws. Although tolerated in many areas, its administration was in very poor state and record-keeping was a low priority. This remained so until 1829 when Catholic Emancipation was achieved.

Ecclesiastical Parishes: Church of Ireland parishes are co-extensive with civil parishes (see map p.15) while Catholic parishes have separate boundaries. Catholic parishes were usually larger than their Church of Ireland counterparts and were regularly reorganised to accommodate changing demographic situations (see map p.32).

Local Guides and Surveys

Below are some useful sources of information on the administration systems, economy, infrastructure, agriculture and people of Donegal.

W. Wilson's, The Post-Chaise Companion, 1786

This guide, intended for the use of travellers, contains more than five hundred pages of descriptions of the great houses, sites of antiquity, manufactures and the rural landscape through which the post-chaise roads pass.

Statistical Survey of County Donegal, 1802

County Surveys were carried out under the direction of the Royal Dublin Society to determine the '*actual state, capabilities and defects of agriculture, manufactures and rural economy*'. They detail conditions in pre-Famine Ireland, including social and economic conditions, the growth of population and poverty, education, religion, history, the Irish language and local customs. The Donegal survey was carried out by James McParlan, a medical doctor. It contains his views on the reasons for the poor condition of many of the rural population, which he firmly blames on the excessive production of whiskey! This book is exceptionally important for Donegal, where information is sparse for the early nineteenth century.

The Statistical Account or Parochial Survey (1814).

Usually referred to as Masons Survey, this was compiled by William Shaw Mason, Secretary to the Board of Public Records and Secretary to the Board of First Fruits. He collected information from the rectors of Donegal parishes on all aspects of life in the county. The section on the inhabitants deals with food, dress and employment while the Gentlemen's seats list the actual occupier of a property, not its owner. An appendix lists the names of the Quarterlands, the Townlands in each, as well as landed proprietor to which they belonged. The rectors who contributed were:

o   Rev. Edward Chichester Culdaff and Clonca
o   Rev. F. L. Molloy Clomany
o   Rev. Alex Montgomery Inver
o   Rev. Henry Major Kilbarron
o   Rev. M. Ingram Templecarn

The Ordnance Survey Memoirs.

In 1824 a committee of the House of Commons recommended a townland survey of Ireland on the six-inch scale as a uniform and equitable valuation for taxation. This survey, which was compiled in the years 1833-1836 does not refer to surnames in Donegal. The Memoirs are the detailed books used by the surveyors containing information on each holding and building.

Samuel Lewis, Topographical Dictionary of Ireland, 3 vols (1st Edition, 1837).

This gives details about every parish, town and village in Ireland, including numbers of inhabitants, the economy, history, topography, religion and parish structures, administration and courts, schools, and much more. It also gives the names of the principal inhabitants (generally landlords, merchants and professionals). (See below.)

> DRUMHOLM, DRIMHOLM, or DRUMHOME, a parish, in the barony of TYRHUGH, county of DONEGAL, and province of ULSTER, 4 miles (N.) from Ballyshannon; containing 8502 inhabitants. St. Ernan, who died about 640, was abbot of a monastery here, where Flahertach O'Maldory, King of Tyrconnell, was buried in 1197. The parish is situated on Donegal bay, and, according to the Ordnance survey, comprises 35,433 statute acres, of which 15,482 are applotted under the tithe act. It is a vicarage, in the diocese of Raphoe, forming the corps of the prebend of Drumholm in Raphoe cathedral, and is in the patronage of the Bishop; the rectory is impropriate in Col. Conolly. The tithes amount to £735. 3. 6¾., of which £245. 1. 2¾. is payable to the impropriator, and the remainder to the vicar. The glebe-house was erected in 1792, by aid of a gift of £100 from the late Board of First Fruits. The glebe comprises 531 plantation acres, of which 400 are cultivated, and the remainder is a rabbit burrow. A church was built at Ballintra, in 1795, at an expense of £1098, of which £500 was a gift from the same Board, and the Ecclesiastical Commissioners have recently granted £252. 13. 9. for its repair. Another church was built at Rossnowlough, in 1830, by aid of a grant of £600 from the late Board of First Fruits, which also granted £350 towards building a chapel at Golard. The R. C. parish is co-extensive with that of the Established Church, and has a large plain chapel near Ballintra. There are places of worship for Presbyterians in connection with the Synod of Ulster, and for Wesleyan Methodists. About 690 children are educated in the public schools, and 20 in a private school; there are also eight Sunday schools.—See BALLINTRA.

Entry from the 'Topographical Dictionary of Ireland' (1837) see p. 18

The Parliamentary Gazetteer of Ireland, 1846

This guide contains more than 2,200 pages of statistical, topographical and anecdotal material on smaller villages and hamlets as well as larger towns and cities. It is available on CD from Archive Books (Dublin) and includes a thorough index.

Tracing Your Donegal Ancestors

Name and Registration District.	Vol.	Page	Name and Registration District.	Vol.	Page
HAVENER, William. Middleton	9	822	HAY, Ellen Jane. Larne	6	658
HAVERAN, Patrick. Killala	19	379	— Helena Mary. Kilkenny	13	515
HAVERN, Ann. Ballymena	11	123	— Isabella. Belfast	1	317
— Mary. Belfast	6	474	— Jane. Gortin	17	127
HAVERON, Jenny. Ballymena	11	147	— John. Belfast	6	286
— William. Newtownlimavady	16	876	— John. Ballymoney	11	165
HAVERTY, Anne. Loughrea	19	419	— John. Belfast	16	349
— Patrick. Glennamaddy	9	327	— Mary Ann. Larne	6	659
— Peter. Glennamaddy	4	366	— Mary Hannah. Dublin, North	12	585
— William. Rathdown	17	864	— Nancy. Ballymoney	11	178
— (male). Cork	10	156	— Sarah. Larne	1	618
— (male). Cork	15	138	— Thomas. Millford	2	306
HAVEY, Owen. Bawnboy	8	67	— William. Millford	7	269
HAVIN, Johanah. Dungarvan	9	695	— William. Larne	11	608
— Patrick. Athlone	8	23	— William. Belfast	1	357
HAVLIN, Mary. Inishowen	12	143	— (female). Millford	2	293
HAVRON, Daniel. Larne	6	663	— (female). Dublin, South	12	748
— Thomas. Ballymena	6	166	HAYBURN, Catherine. Larne	16	596
— William. Larne	16	584	HAYDE, Mary. Cashel	13	469
HAW, Elizabeth. Magherafelt	11	749	— Mary. Naas	2	975
— Jeremiah. Fermoy	19	782	HAYDEN, Agnes. Strokestown	3	420
— Margaret Jane. Magherafelt	11	773	— Alexander. Enniscorthy	9	717
— Margaret Jane. Magherafelt	6	864	— Andrew. Enniscorthy	4	821
— Mary. Waterford	14	882	— Anne. Thomastown	14	858
— Richard. Cookstown	11	513	— Anne. Dublin, North	7	642
— Richard. Cookstown	11	511	— Bridget. Urlingford	3	811
HAWE, Bridget. New Ross	14	817	— Catherine. Carlow	13	458
— Honora. Kanturk	20	275	— Catherine. Thomastown	14	845
— James. Lisburn	16	655	— Catherine. Carlow	13	456
— John. Fermoy	14	743	— Christina Mary. Dublin, South	17	734
— Letitia. Bailieborough	12	409	— Cornelius. Tipperary	13	645
— Margaret. Mallow	5	610	— Dora. Gorey	17	793
— Margaret. Kilkenny	3	599	— Edward Francis Joseph. Dublin, North	2	689
— Mary. Fermoy	9	773	— Elizabeth Emily. Balrothery	2	495
— Michael. Callan	10	648	— Ellen. Carlow	3	486
— Richard. Callan	9	608	— Ellen. Cashel	8	553
HAWSS, Kate. Ballyvaughan	9	65	— Ellen. Baltinglass	2	517
HAWEY, Catherine. Tobercurry	4	608	— Ellen. Dublin, South	7	736
HAWISY, Mary Ann. Dundalk	7	845	— James. Shillelagh	17	935
HAWK, George. Celbridge	2	545	— James. Callan	14	603
HAWKES, Claude Somerville. Rathdown	17	888	— James Michael. Dublin, North	17	598
— Emma Teresa. Macroom	15	452	— Jeremiah. Athy	18	405
— Frances Caroline. Bandon	15	21	— John. Enniscorthy	19	745
— Johanna. Bandon	20	11	— John. Roscommon	13	350
— Timothy. Bandon	15	4	— John. New Ross	14	840
— William. Bandon	10	11	— John. Rathdrum	7	1049
HAWKING, Levinia Eva. Castletown	5	86	— John. Rathdrum	17	912
HAWKINS, Anne. Wexford	9	965	— John. Rathdown	12	897
— Bridget. Gort	14	343	— Laurence. Thurles	13	638
— Catherine. Baltinglass	7	479	— Margaret. Thomastown	9	897
— Elizabeth. Wexford	4	1057	— Margaret. Dublin, South	17	621
— Elizabeth Mary. Waterford	14	881	— Mary. Waterford	9	940
— Ellen. Galway	9	308	— Mary. Callan	9	599
— Hannah. Ennis	4	281	— Mary. Enniscorthy	4	821
— James. Dublin, South	12	755	— Mary. Kilkenny	8	608
— James. Carlow	8	504	— Mary. Dublin, South	7	765
— James. Fermoy	4	842	— Mary Anne. Dublin, South	17	709
— James. Baltinglass	17	436	— Mary Elizabeth. Dublin, South	7	818
— James. Clogheen	9	652	— Mary Elizabeth. Dublin, North	12	568
— John. Wexford	19	966	— Michael. Thurles	8	734
— Mary. Ennis	9	248	— Michael. Waterford	14	881
— Mary. Glin	20	246	— Michael. Nenagh	13	563

A section of a page from the Index to Births Registered in Ireland in 1866. The format for the indexes to marriages and deaths is similar, however the index to deaths also includes the age at death.

Chapter 4 Civil Registration

The civil registration of Irish births, marriages and deaths of all denominations began in 1864. Church of Ireland marriages had been registered from 1845. The administration set up for this purpose involved appointment of registrars in districts based on the Poor Law Unions (see p. 16). Each district compiled its own records, which were then sent to the General Register Office (GRO) in Dublin where the records for the whole country were stored. An index for each year is available at the GRO, and an index to the records of each district is held in the respective District Office.

Although a system for registration of all births was established in 1864 there was no penalty for not registering until 1874. Births in particular may not have been registered as Catholics considered this less important than having their children baptised. Thus RC baptism records are probably more comprehensive than civil records.

All certificates state the county, Registration District and the Superintendent Registrar's District. The Superintendent Registrar's District corresponds with the old Poor Law Union. The Registration District corresponds to the old Dispensary District within the PLU. When consulting the GRO indexes for a birth entry etc, it is important to know the PLU within which the event may have been registered. The 'Index to the Townlands and Towns' (see p. 16) indicates the PLU within which each townland is located and therefore the Superintendent Registrar's District within which a registered event should be sought.

The details available on each form of record are:

Birth Certificate: States the forename and surname of the child, the date and place of birth and date of registration. The name of the father, his address and occupation; name and maiden name of the mother; name and address of the person registering the birth.

Marriage Certificate: States the date and place of the marriage (including name of the church). The pre-marriage names, ages, occupations and addresses of the bride and groom, and their 'condition' (e.g. bachelor, widow etc). It also states the names and occupations of the fathers of the bride and groom (also indicating if either is deceased); and of the witnesses and officiating clergyman. In many cases, the ages will be specified only as 'full age' (i.e. over 21).

Death Certificate: States the name of the deceased and the age, occupation, condition and cause of death. It also states the date and place of death and the name and address of the person registering the death.

In the case of all three types of certificates it is worth bearing in mind that the information is only as accurate as was given by the contributors.

Copies of certificates can be obtained from the General Register Office (GRO). The main GRO office is located in Roscommon, but there are local offices in every county (see www.groireland.ie for details) and there is a public search room in the Dublin office (see p. 147). Copies of certificates can also be obtained from this office. The fee schedule is on the above website. The GRO staff will conduct limited searches for an event if you can provide a reasonably exact year for its occurrence, but will not conduct general research on your behalf.

In 1894 the Registrar General, Robert Matheson, published a study on the occurrence of Family names in Ireland entitled 'Special Report on Surnames in Ireland' (see p. 23). Reprint, 1994: Genealogical Publishing Co., Inc., Baltimore, MD. It is based on births in 1890 where there were five or more occurrences of a particular surname. In a series of tables Irish surnames are dissected into 'numerical strength, derivation, ethnology and distribution'.

Other records held at the GRO
• Army Births, Marriages and Deaths
• Births and Deaths at Sea
• Boer War
• British Consular Births and Deaths
• Great War Deaths
• Schulze Register

TABLE showing the SURNAMES IN IRELAND having Five Entries and upwards in the Birth Indexes of 1890, together with the Number in each Registration Province, and the Registration Counties in which these Names are principally found—*continued*.

Names.	NUMBER OF ENTRIES IN BIRTH INDEXES FOR 1890.					Counties in which principally found
	IRELAND.	Leinster.	Munster.	Ulster.	Connaught.	
*McErlain (11)—McErlean (8),	21	–	–	21	–	13 in Antrim and 8 in Derry.
*McEvoy (85),	99	54	6	36	3	Dublin, Louth, Armagh, and Queen's.
*McFadden (72),	79	2	1	73	3	Donegal, Antrim, and Londonderry.
*McFall (20),	24	1	–	23	–	16 in Antrim and 7 in Londonderry.
McFarland,	46	2	–	44	–	Tyrone and Armagh.
*McFarlane (7),	12	4	–	8	–	—
*McFeeters (6),	7	–	–	7	–	Londonderry.
McFerran,	7	1	–	6	–	6 in Antrim.
*McFetridge (8),	9	–	–	9	–	6 in Antrim and 3 in Londonderry.
McGahan,	13	7	–	6	–	7 in Louth.
*McGahey (12),	13	–	–	13	–	Antrim and Monaghan.
*McGann (18),	21	9	3	3	6	—
*McGarry (64),	79	21	–	29	29	Antrim, Dublin, Roscommon, and Leitrim—very few elsewhere.
*McGarvey (28),	30	1	–	29	–	18 in Donegal and 5 in Londonderry.
McGaughey,	7	–	–	7	–	3 in Antrim and 3 in Armagh.
McGeady,	5	–	–	5	–	All in Donegal.
McGeary,	8	1	–	7	–	Tyrone.
*McGeehan (7),	11	–	–	11	–	9 in Donegal.
McGeough,	11	3	–	8	–	Monaghan and Louth.
McGeown,	19	2	–	17	–	12 in Armagh.
McGettigan,	10	–	–	10	–	All in Donegal.
McGillicuddy,	6	–	6	–	–	All in Kerry.
*McGilloway (8),	10	–	–	10	–	5 in Londonderry and 5 in Donegal.
McGimpsey,	8	–	–	8	–	7 in Down and 1 in Antrim.
McGing,	10	–	–	–	10	7 in Mayo and 2 in Leitrim.
*McGinley (45),	47	–	–	46	1	57 in Donegal.
*McGinn (17)—Maginn (13),	31	4	–	25	2	Generally distributed in Ulster.
*McGinty (10),	12	–	1	9	2	Donegal.
McGirr,	12	1	–	9	2	Tyrone.
*McGivern (17),	18	–	–	18	–	7 in Armagh, 7 in Down, and 4 in Antrim.
McGivney,	6	–	–	6	–	All in Cavan.
McGlade,	8	1	–	7	–	Antrim and Londonderry.
*McGlinchey (17),	22	–	–	22	–	Tyrone and Donegal.
*McGloin (14),	16	1	–	7	8	Donegal and Sligo.
McGlone,	12	–	–	11	1	Tyrone.
*McGlynn (26),	39	9	3	16	11	—
McGoey,	5	2	–	1	2	—
*McGoldrick (34),	41	3	1	26	11	Tyrone, Fermanagh, and Sligo.
*McGonigle (24),	38	–	–	38	–	Donegal and Londonderry.
McGookin,	7	–	–	7	–	5 in Antrim and 2 in Armagh.
*McGough (8),	11	2	–	1	8	Mayo.
McGourty,	5	–	–	2	3	Leitrim.
*McGovern (92),	102	13	1	65	23	Fermanagh, Cavan, and Leitrim.
*McGowan (112)—Magowan (28),	152	5	2	91	54	Donegal, Leitrim, and Sligo.

A page from 'Special Report on Surnames in Ireland' by Robert E. Matheson.
The report was published as an appendix to the 29th Report of the Registrar-General in 1894.

The Church of Jesus Christ of Latter Day Saints (LDS)

The LDS have been collecting genealogical information worldwide since 1894 and their records include millions of baptism, birth and marriage records. Access to the majority of the LDS material is free either on the net or at their Family History Centres. Since 1948 the LDS have been microfilming Irish genealogical records, including birth, baptism, and marriage records. However not all Irish registers were covered as the LDS were only granted restricted access. The LDS have microfilms of both the GRO indexes and a selection of certificates at their Family History Centres. These records can be obtained on their website www.familysearch.org/. The LDS Family History Centre in Ireland is located at Finglas Road, Dublin 9 (see p. 148).

A useful resource produced by the LDS is the International Genealogical Index (IGI). It is on microfiche and the website and the access points are surname, country and county. It includes GRO births and marriages, and details from baptism and marriage registers. It is useful in tracing uncommon surnames and ascertaining the counties and parishes where a particular surname is concentrated.

Index to Irish Marriages:
An index to marriages from 1771 to 1812 was published in *Walker's Hibernian Magazine* in 1897. It was reprinted in 1992 and 1996 by the Clearfield Publishing company. An index to births, marriages and deaths published in Anthologia Hibernica 1793 to 1794 is also included in the back section of the book. This book is available in the NLI and the Dublin City Library and Archive, and from the above publishers.

Marriage Licence Bonds.
During the seventeenth and eighteen centuries, when it was illegal for 'dissenting' ministers to perform marriages, some Roman Catholic and Presbyterians chose to be married in the Church of Ireland. To do so they would ask the minister to publish banns (i.e. a public notice of the marriage) or purchase a licence from the Bishop of the diocese. Before the licence was granted the couple had to enter a bond (i.e. a sum of money as a surety) at a diocesan court. Only the index to these bonds survive, but they include the names of the bride and groom and their ages and place of residence.

For bonds for the diocese of Raphoe see Rosemary ffolliott, *Index to Raphoe Marriage Licence Bonds, 1710-1755 and 1817-1830* (Dublin 1969, supplement to the Irish Ancestor. The Raphoe Bonds (1660-1750) are available in the NAI (and in LDS Film 100872) and those for Clogher diocese (1709 only) are in PRONI -1088 MIC/5B/4; NAI; and LDS film 100861.

Chapter 5 Censuses and Census Substitutes

This chapter contains a list of sources of information on persons resident in Donegal. They were compiled for a huge range of different religious, legal and administrative purposes, but are very useful as they act as 'substitute' censuses in the absence of formal census information. National censuses of population for Ireland were compiled at ten year intervals from 1821. Although statistical and analytical information is available for the 19th century census returns, the only complete household returns are for the censuses of 1901 and 1911. The census returns for 1861, 1871, 1881 and 1891 were pulped by government order during the 19th century, while almost all of those for 1821, 1831, 1841 and 1851 were burned in the Public Record fire in 1921. Some of the census returns survived the fire, but none were from Co. Donegal.

It should also be noted that, in the period from 1908 (when old age pensions were introduced) and 1921, family information had been extracted from the 1841 and 1851 census returns. This was done to validate the age of pension claimants. This limited material was not stored in the Public Record Office and survives intact. A selection of census substitutes and census returns for Co. Donegal is presented below and is divided thus:

A. Deals with Census/Census Substitutes that deal with the entire county.
B. Sources that deal with parts of the county.

A. Census Substitutes that deal with all of the county

1612 - 13 Undertakers: Lists of English and Scottish landlords granted land in Donegal (Hist. Mss Commission Rept. No. 4 - Hasting Mss) NAI.

1618 Muster Roll: Able bodied men at arms   PRONI MIC637/10 (D/1759/3B/5)

1622 Ulster Inquisitions: 1622 –V. Treadwell in Don. Ann. Vol. 2 (1951-4) and Vol 3 (1954-7). This material is also available in "The

Irish Commission of 1622: an investigation of the Irish administration 1615-1622 and its consequences 1623-1624" by Victor Treadwell, IMC (2006).

1630 Muster Roll: Lists of major landlords and of the able-bodied men at arms (16-60 years) they could muster. The surnames are reflective of the plantation ethnic population of English and Scots in Co. Donegal (NLI m/f P. 206; Don Ann 10(2) (1972) & DCL. Also available at www. ulsterancestry.com/ua-free-Muster_Rolls_Donegal_1631.html

1630-31 Muster Roll: Able bodied men at arms PRONI MIC637/10 (D/1759/3C/2) and Don. Ann. 1972.

1640-1688 Books of Survey and Distribution: These books list the owners of land before and after the confiscations of the 1650s and the Act of Settlement and Explanations of the 1660s plus the forfeitures of 1688. Books are divided by county and parish. Published by the Irish Manuscripts Commission. Also in Annesley Collection PRONI – D/1854/1 and MIC/532.

1654 Civil Survey: These are records of land ownership compiled between 1654-1656. They are more detailed than the Books of Survey and Distribution and contain topographical and descriptive features, wills, and deeds. (IMC. Vol III, I 6551) & DCL.

1659 Census of Ireland: Lists of people entitled to land or 'tituladoes'. Divided into respective baronies, parishes and townlands. It also lists the number of Irish, Scots and English in each townland; the principal surnames and their frequency. Published in '*Census of Ireland c1659*' ed. by Seamus Pender (National Manuscripts Commission, 1939); also in NLI Ir 31041 c 4 and DCL. Also freely available on the web.

1663 Hearth Money Rolls: See entry below. NAI mf 2473 and PRONI T808/15003.

1665 Hearth Money Rolls: Lists those liable to pay a tax based on the number of hearths (fireplaces) per house. Lists the head of household in each barony, parish and townland. NLI. ms 958314 & GO 538; PRONI. T283D/ T307D & T 307C; DCL; LDS films 100181 & 258502 [also listed in '*The Laggan and its Presbyterianism*' by Lecky, A.G. Belfast 1905].

1704-1839 The Convert Rolls: It lists the name, date of conversion and some addresses and other information of Catholics who converted to the Church of Ireland during the Penal Times. Published in several volumes. The Convert Rolls Eileen O'Byrne, IMC Dublin, 1981 and also O'Byrne, E., editor, The Convert Rolls; The Calendar of the Convert Rolls, 1703-1838; Chamney, Anne, editor, Fr. Wallace Clare's Annotated List of Converts, 1703-78, IMC Dublin, 2005. A total of almost 8,000 names but few from Donegal.

1662-1666 Subsidy Rolls: These list the nobility, clergy and laity who paid a grant in aid to the Crown. They include the name of the taxpayer, amount paid and the status of the person. Because they include only the wealthier members of society, they are less useful than hearth money rolls. Ref. for 1662 (PRONI T808/14998) and 1666 (PRONI T808/15003).

1760-1769 Freeholders Lists: A list of land-occupiers who held land for life as distinct from leaseholders and annual rent payers. They were a major group entitled to vote. NLI m/f P. 975; PRONI. T 808/14999; DCL.

1761-1788 Freeholder Lists: NLI. ms. 787/8

1761 Militia List: Co.Donegal.
GO ms 680. (see also 1808).

1761-1775: Poll Book (list of those entitled to vote): Co. Donegal. LDS mf 100181, GO ms 442, PRONI (T/808/14999, mf 353/1).

1770 Freeholders Entitled to Vote: NLI. ms 987-88.

1775-81 List of Freeholders: PRONI T/808/15006 (see also 1789-90)

1789-90 List of Freeholders: PRONI T/808/15006

1796 Spinning Wheel Premium Entitlement Lists: To encourage the linen industry the Irish Linen Board awarded free spinning wheels or looms to people growing certain acreages of flax. The names of those given spinning wheels are listed. (see sample entries on p.28). NLI ir 63341117; PRONI MF/7/1; NAI; DCL and on CD from Family Tree Maker.

Prfh. of **KILLCAR**				
	Wheels	William Humphries	-	-	1
Thomas Carfaddin	- - 1	Manus M'Corkill	- - 1
Daniel M'Breartey	- - 1	Owen Doolan	- - 1
Charles M'Breartey	- - 1	Widow Tunney	- - 1
John Cochran	- - 1	James Tunney	- - 1
Andrew Gartlay	- - 1	Andrew Sweeney	- - 1
Charles M'Breartey	- - 1	Patrick Bannagan	- - 1
John Carfaddin	- - 1	Daniel Afh	- - 1
Thomas Lenaghan	- - 1	William Kerrigan	- - 1
Denis Cannon	- - 1	Francis Moore	- - 1
Patrick M'Breartey	- - 1	Edward Kelly	- - 1
Charles M'Fadden	- - 1	John Kelly	- - 1
James Cannon	- - 1	Daniel Dougherty	- - 1
Conniel M'Intire	- - 1	James Gallaugher	- - 1
Denis Cannon	- - 1	John Hills	- - 1
		Owen Hills	- - 1

An abstract from the Spinning Wheel Premiums Entitlements Lists

1799 Muster Roll: PRONI T.115B.

1800 Petitions Relating to the Act of Union: The Act of Union (1800) abolished the Irish parliament and henceforth Irish MPs represented their consituents at Westminster. During the debates associated with this, petitions both for and against were submitted. Several such petitions for Donegal were published in the *Belfast Newsletter* on the following dates: 27 & 31 Dec 1799 and 3, 7 & 17 Jan 1800.

1808 Militia List: Co.Donegal.
John Watson Stewart's Almanack of 1808

1820-1830's Tithe Applotment Books: Tithes were a tax levied by the Church of Ireland on all occupiers of land from 1823. The 'Books' list those liable to pay, the amount payable and the acreage of land. People are listed in their parish and townland. NAI. m/f; Gilbert Library m/f, Dublin.

1831 National Schools Pupil Registers: (See Chap. 12 National Schools).

1839 Game Certificates: List of persons who obtained game certificates in Ulster, PRONI T.686, LDS mf 100179.

1843 Voters List: NAI OP2 1843/56.

1857 Griffith's Primary Valuation of Tenements: (See Chap. 7 Land and Estate Records)

1876 Land Owners in Ireland: Return of owners of land of one acre and upwards, in several Counties, cities and towns in Ireland. Dublin, 1876. Reprinted Baltimore 1988.

1878 The Landowners of Ireland by O.H. Hussey de Burgh (1878) lists major landowners, and size and location of their holdings.

1901 Government Census: The original returns list all persons living in every household. Personal details include name, surname, age, relationship (e.g. Wife) married or single, religion, occupation, place born (county or town), ability to read, write and speak English and Irish. NAI; DCL (m/film).

1908-1921 Old Age Pension Claims: When pensions were introduced in 1908, persons over 70 years had to prove their age to obtain the pension. As there were no birth certs, the 1841 and 1851 census returns were often consulted by PRO staff, and these search results survive. As well as claimant's details, claimant's family information may also be recorded. These are held at NAI and PRONI. Claimants from Inishowen barony can be found at the PRONI (T.550, Vol 37).

1911 Government Census: Includes the same details as the 1901 Census (see above) and also (a) how many years each listed couple were married and (b) how many children were born to them and how many survived. NAI; This census will be made available in digital form on the NAI website in 2010 approximately. DCL (m/film).

1912 Signatures of Covenant: Signatories of a covenant/petition against the granting of Home Rule on Ulster Day, 28th September 1912. PRONI D1098/1 Boxes 33-39. Archives – web www.PRONI.gov.uk.

1936 Electoral Registers: In bound volume form. These include all citizens of 21 years and over in their respective townlands or street addresses. NLI and DCL.

1898-1959 Electoral Registers: Available in Donegal County Archives CC/14/2

B. Census Substitutes that deal with part of the county

1608 Land Grants: Notes on leases and tenants for Raphoe Barony. In Hill's "Plantation of Ulster" Belfast (1877).

1613 Settlers in Co. Donegal: About **1613** Leases given to early English and Scottish settlers in the area known as the Laggan. Lists lessors and c. 115 tenants. www.ulsterancestry.com and DCL.

1614 Early Tenants: (English and Scottish) of Donegal estates – names and townlands. Published in *The Laggan and Its Presbyterianism*. Lecky A.G. Belfast 1905. [Appendix A].

1642 Muster Roll of Sir. Robert Stewart's regiment at Raphoe, County Donegal, 1642- T/808/15166. LDS mf 897012.

1643 Muster Roll: Col. Audley Mervyn's muster roll at Ellagh, Co Donegal. PRONI T808/15177

1664 Lifford Petition: Petition of parishioners of Lifford [sic] to Bishop of Derry about the parish schoolmaster, 1664 (80 signatories) – PRONI D/683/163; (also in T. W. Moody and J. G. Simms, *The Bishopric of Derry and the Irish Society of London,* 1602-1705 (2 vols, Dublin, 1968-83)

1669 Subsidy Roll: Kilmacrenan, Raphoe, Taughboyne and Tirhugh (PRONI T.307; LDS mf 258502,).

1691-1703 Williamite Land Settlement: Following the end of the Williamite War in1691, lands confiscated from defeated Jacobites were forfeited and given to William's followers. These records include Parish of All Saints in Donegal. PRONI D/1854.

1740 Protestant Householders: Forenames and surnames of Protestant householders in townlands of the parishes of Clonmany, Culdaff, Desertegney, Donagh, Fawne (Fahan), Moville, Templemore (Mintiaghs or Barr of Inch). GO 539; PRONI T808/15258.

1745 Muster Roll of Abercorn Estate: Printed in the journal of Irish Family History Research 21 (1998).

1766 Religious Census: A census conducted by Church of Ireland clergy.It generally contains little information on Catholics. Available for parishes of: Donaghmore NAI mf 207/8. Also Census of Protestants of Inch and Leck: DCL; NAI 1A 41 100; on shelves of public search room in PRONI and in *"The Laggan and its Presbyterianism"* Lecky. A.G. Belfast 1905; Raphoe – NAI M2476.

1773 Murlog Church Baptisms (Clonleigh Parish): Photocopy in DCL

1782 Inhabitants of Culdaff Parish: In 'Three Hundred Years in Inishowen', A. Young 1929.

1794 Householders in St. Johnston and tenants on Donegal Abercorn Estates (LKL): Census of Protestants in Leck parish and householders in St.Johnston (Taughboyne parish) in 'The Laggan and its Presbyterianism' Lecky, A.G. Belfast 1905.

1796 Clondavaddog Parish Census: Protestant Baptisms, Marriages and Deaths. PRONI M1C/1/164A

1799 Templecrone Parish Protestant Householders: In 'Irish Ancestor' 16(2) 1984.

1802-1803 Culdaff Parish Protestant Census: In 'Three Hundred Years in Inishowen' A. Young. 1929.

1852-1864 Vaccination Register: Milford NLI ms 9767 (child's name, age, date of vaccination).

1852-1872 Vaccination Register: Rathmullan. NLI ms. 9975 (see above).

1857 St. Eunan's RC Marriages: List of Marriages in St. Eunan's RC Church Letterkenny. DCL

1878 Inhabitants List: List of families in Parish of Conwall compiled by W. Craig. DCL

1875-1902 Inhabitants List: Conwall (some with years of birth) RCBL P.206/8/1a.

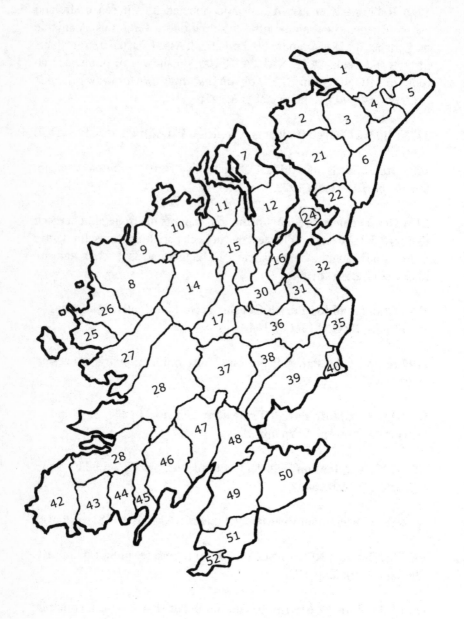

Map of Roman Catholic Parishes (see pages 35 - 37)

Chapter 6 Church Records

Church records, such as registers of baptisms, marriages and burials, are invaluable when making a family tree as they usually pre-date the initiation of civil registration in 1864. Vestry minutes, account books, etc., although not a feature of Catholic records, can be equally useful, especially as they often pre-date even the above registers. The 1861 Government Census showed that Donegal residents were 75% Catholic; 12.6% Protestant; 11% Presbyterian and 1% Methodist (see p. 39). Records of all these Churches exist, and are the only record of the existence of many, if not most of the people of Donegal. These records are discussed below, and sources of the records for each parish are also provided.

Catholic Church Records

Although Roman Catholicism was the religion of the majority of the people of Donegal, the Catholic Church was severely repressed during the 18th century by a series of 'Penal Laws'. It was only at the close of that century that a relaxation of these laws occurred and a process of church-building and parish administration began.

The practical consequences of this for family history are that Catholic churches were poorer and less well organised. Significant factors determining whether churches kept records included the wealth of the parish, and the competence and inclination of the priests and bishops to keep records. In general larger towns have the earliest parish registers and rural registers start later. A full description of the factors affecting record keeping is given in 'Irish Church Records' (Flyleaf Press 2001).

In comparison with other Irish counties, Donegal Catholic records start relatively late, the majority start in the mid 19th century. The earliest registers are for Clonleigh and Urney dating from 1773. The records also vary widely in legibility and are written in Latin or English, never in Irish. Baptismal registers give the name of the child, the names of the father and mother, date and place of Baptism, and the godparents. The occupation of the father and date of birth of the child may sometimes be given. Marriage registers give less information – see paragraph on the Church of Ireland records. Unlike the Church of Ireland the Roman Catholic Church often kept no burial registers – some of those kept are actually recording of "offerings" (funeral dues) paid at the funeral of the deceased.

The National Library of Ireland (NLI) microfilmed the majority of Catholic registers in the 1950s and these microfilms are accessible in the Library. In the NLI index to microfilms they are organised by diocese, and it is therefore useful to know the diocese to which each parish of interest belongs. Derry and Raphoe dioceses cover all of Donegal except for two parishes, which are in Clogher diocese.

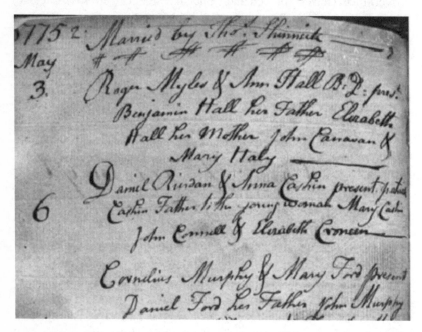

A typical entry from a Roman Catholic church marriage register

The Catholic parishes of Donegal are listed from the next page, together with a reference number indicating their position on the map on page 32. The most recent parishes were formed from older parishes in the same geographical area. In these cases the map reference numbers are the same. The baptism, marriage and burial registers are extant from the date stated and can be found in one or all of the archival centres listed. The registers listed here are those, which start before 1895.

Roman Catholic Church Registers (see p. 32 for map of parishes)

Parish	Map Ref.	Baptisms	Marriage	Burials	Location
All Saints or Killea or Taughboyne	32	1843	1843		NLI/DAL /DGC
Annagry	26	1868			NLI
Ardara	28	1868	1867		NLI/DAL
Arranmore Island	25	1886	1887		DAL
Aughnish & Aghanunshin	16	1873	1873	1873	NLI/DAL
Ballyfin	28	1890		1894	DAL
Burt	22	1859	1856	1860	NLI/DGC
Cam	50	1851	1836		NLI
Churchill	14	1884	1920		DAL
Clonca	1	1856	1870		NLI/DAL
Clondahorky	10	1877	1879		NLI
Clondavaddog	7	1847	1847	1847	NLI/DAL
Clonleigh	35	1773	1778		NLI/DGC/PRONI
Clonmany	2	1852	1852		NLI/DGC
Conwal & Leck	30	1853	1853		NLI/DAL
Culdaff	4	1838	1849		NLI/DAL

Parish	Map ref.	Baptisms	Marriages	Burials	Location
Desertegny	21	1864	1871		NLI/DGC
Donagh	3	1847	1849		NLI/DGC
Donaghmore	39	1840	1846		NLI
Drumholm	49	1866	1866		NLI/DAL
Drumkeen (Raphoe)	-	1893	1893		DAL
Dunfanaghy	15	1856	1856		DAL
Falcarragh	10	1889	1887		DAL
Gartan & Termon	14	1862			NLI/DAL
Glencolumcille	42	1879	1881		NLI/DAL
Glenswilly	17	1874	1877		DAL
Glenvar	12	1888	1843		DAL
Gortahork	9	1849	1861		NLI
Gweedore	8	1868	1866		NLI/DAL
Inishkeel	28	1866	1866		NLI/DAL
Innishmacsaint	52	1848	1847		NLI
Inver	46	1861	1861		NLI/DAL
Iskaheen	6	1858			NLI/DGC
Kilbarron	51	1854	1858		NLI/DAL
Kilcar	43	1848			NLI/DAL
Kilclonney	28	1885			DAL
Kilmacrenan	15	1862	1863		NLI/DAL

Parish	Map ref.	Baptisms	Marriages	Burials	Location
Killaghtee	45	1845	1857		NLI/DAL
Killybegs	44	1850	1850		NLI/DAL
Killygarvan & Tullyfern	12	1868	1873		NLI/DAL
Killymard	47	1874			NLI/DAL
Kincasslagh	25	1877	1878		DAL
Kilteevogue	37	1855	1855		NLI/DAL
Lettermacward & Templecrone	27	1876	1877		NLI/DAL
Mevagh	11	1871	1878		NLI/DAL
Milford	12	1874	1885		DAL
Moville Lr	5	1847	1847	1847	NLI/DGC
NewtonCunningham	32	1857			DAL
Raphoe	36	1876	1876		NLI/DAL
Rathmullan	12	1859	1873		DAL
Stranorlar	38	1860	1877		NLI/DAL
Tawnawilly	48	1872	1882		DAL
Tullaghobegley/ Raymunterdoney	9	1868			NLI
Raymoghy	31	1854	1855		DAL
Tory Is. & Urney	40	1773			NLI

The Convert Rolls 1703-1838.

The convert rolls list those converting from Roman Catholicism to Protestantism (limited to the Church of Ireland). Following the 'Act to prevent further growth of popery' of 1703, a Catholic converting to the Church of Ireland had to provide proof of conformity. By Confirming to the Established Church a Catholic was freed from the legal disabilities affecting property rights and membership of certain professions, etc in force under the Penal Laws.

The original rolls were destroyed in Dublin in 1922, but not before they had been calendared and recorded. The Convert Rolls were published by the Irish Manuscripts Commission in 1981 under the editorship of Eileen O'Byrne. This has been updated by A. Chamney in 2005.

The rolls give the date of conformity, the name and address of the convert, and date. Occasionally the occupation of the convert is given also.

Church of Ireland Records

It is important to understand that after the Treaty of Mellifont (1603) the Church of Ireland (also known as Protestant, Episcopal or Anglican Church) was the State or Established Church and continued as such until 1869. As the 'Established Church', it was effectively an arm of government and had jurisdiction over Will probate, marriage and some other functions. Its clergy often held important positions within the community and its churches were at one time the only churches where worship was formally allowed. Its graveyards were also the legal resting place not only for Church of Ireland parishioners but also those of other denominations. However, despite the benefits of affiliation to the Church of Ireland, the Penal Laws did not result in the conversion of more than a small fraction of the native population of Donegal. The non-Catholic population was mainly those of Scottish or English descent. A full account of the records of the Church of Ireland is given by Raymond Refausse in *Irish Church Records* (Flyleaf Press 2001).

In 1869 the Church of Ireland was disestablished, i.e. ceased to be the State Church. As their records were State records, the PRO took charge of the baptism and burial registers prior to 1870 and the marriage registers prior to 1845. From 1845 the Registrar General had supplied pro-forma marriage registers to all Protestant churches to facilitate State registration of marriage. (see Civil Registration - Chapter 4).

In 1922 the PRO burned down, and almost all of the 1,006 registers from Church of Ireland parishes in the building were destroyed. However 637 parishes still retained the records in their own custody and other parishes had copied their registers before depositing them with the PRO.

County Donegal has a fairly good collection of Church of Ireland registers in comparison with other counties. The earliest are those for Drumholm, which date from 1691. The majority of registers however date from the 19th century and all are written in English.

	% Roman Catholic	% Church of Ireland	% Presbyterian	% Methodist
The percentage of members of each of the major religious denominations in the province of Ulster in the Census of 1861 (Population: 1,914,236)				
Antrim	27.5	20.2	47.6	2.4
Armagh	48.8	30.9	16.2	3.2
Cavan	80.5	14.9	3.5	0.9
Derry	45.3	16.9	35.1	0.6
Donegal	**75.1**	**12.6**	**11.0**	**1.0**
Down	32.3	20.5	44.5	1.4
Fermanagh	56.5	38.4	1.8	3.3
Tyrone	56.5	21.9	19.5	1.6
Monaghan	73.4	14.0	12.0	0.3

Extract from 'Irish Church Records'
- Their history availability and use in family and local history.
edited by James G. Ryan (Flyleaf Press, 2001)

Church of Ireland Registers (see p. 14-15 for map of parishes)

Parish	Map ref,	Baptisims	Marriages	Burials	Location of records or copies
All Saints	29	1877	1845	1820	DAL
Ardara	41	1829	1829	1830	DAL/RCBL/LC
Aghanunshin	18	1878	1845	1878	RCBL
Burt	25	1809	1809	1809	DAL/RCBL/LC
Clonca	1	1669	1783		JAPMD, Vol V, No.3(1903)
Clondahorky E	10	1871	1845	1884	DAL/RCBL
Clondahorky W	10	1873	1873		DAL
Clondavaddog	7	1794	1794	1794	DAL/LC
Clonleigh	35	1872	1845	1877	RCBL
Convoy	17	1876	1845	1878	RCBL
Craigadooish	-	1871			RCBL
Culdaff	4	1668-1790	1713-21	1714-18	PRONI
		1875	1845	1876	RCBL
Desertegny	20	1790	1813	1803	DAL/RCBL/LC
Donaghmore	39	1818	1817	1825	DAL/RCBL
Donegal	48	1808	1812	1812	DAL/LC
Drumholme	49	1691	1691	1696	DAL/LC/PRONI
Dunfanaghy	10	1873	1875	1873	DAL

Parish	Map ref.	Baptisms	Marriages	Burials	Location of records or copies
Dunlewey	8		1853	1853	RCBL/LC
Fahan Lwr.	21	1817	1817	1822	DAL/RCBL
Fahan Upr.	22	1762	1765	1765	DAL/RCBL/LC/PRONI
Finner	52	1815	1815	1815	LC
Gartan	14		1881	1845	RCBL
Glenalla	16	1871	1871	1906	DAL/RCBL
Glencolumcille	42	1827	1845	1827	DAL/RCBL/LC
Gleneely	39	1872	1859		RCBL
Glenties	28	1827	1856	1898	DAL/RCBL/LC
Goland C.of Ease	39		1847		DAL
Gweedore	8	1880	1855	1881	DAL/RCBL
Inch	24	1868	1846	1868	DAL/RCBL
Inniskeel	28	1699-1700	1699-1700	1699-1700	NAI/PRONI
		1818	1818	1818	NAI/DAL/LC
		1852	1821	1852	DAL/RCBL
Inishmacsaint	52	1660-72	1663-72	1662-72	PRONI
Inver	46	1805	1805	1818	DAL/DCL/LC
Kilbarron	51	1785	1785	1785	LC/PRONI
Kilcar	43	1819	1819	1818	DAL/RCBL/LC

Parish	Map ref.	Baptisims	Marriages	Burials	Location of records or copies
Killaghtee	45	1775	1758	1762	DAL/LC (DCL from 1857)
Killea	33	1877	1845	1880	DAL/RCBL
Kilteevogue	37	1818	1845	1825	RCBL/LC
Killybegs	41/44	1787	1809	1806	DAL/RCBL/DCL/LC
Killygarvan	13	1706	1706	1706	DAL
Killymard	47	1880	1845	1819	DAL
Laghey (Tyrone)	-	1877	1847	1877	DAL
Leck	30	1878	1846	1878	RCBL
Lettermacward	27	1889	1846	1890	DAL/RCBL
Lough Eske	47	1876			DAL
Meenglass	-	1864			RCBL
Mevagh	11	1876	1846	1877	DAL
Milford	12	1879	1860		DAL/RCBL
Monellan	39	1872	1874	1885	DAL
Mount Charles	46	1877	1861	1860	DAL/ DCL
Muff	23	1803	1804	1847	RCBL/LC
Newtown Cunningham	29	1877	1845	1820	RCBL
Raphoe	34	1771	1771	1771	DAL/PRONI
Raymoghy	31	1844	1845	1878	RCBL

Parish	Map ref.	Baptisms	Marriages	Burials	Location of records or copies
Raymunterdoney	9	1878	1845	1880	DAL
Rossnowlagh	49	1879	1845	1821	DAL
Stranorlar	38	1802	1821	1821	DAL/RCBL/LC
Taughboyne	32	1820	1820	1820	RCBL/LC
Templecarn	50	1825	1825	1825	RCBL/LC
Templecrone	26	1878	1849	1851	RCBL/DAL/LC
Tullaghobegley	8	1821	1821	1850	DAL/LC
Tullaughnish	16	1798	1788	1798	DAL/RCBL/LC

In his *"Researching Scots-Irish Ancestors"*, William J. Roulston of the Ulster Historical Foundation has written *"Analysis of the Church of Ireland Registers has shown that many people who belonged to other denominations frequently appear in these records. There are various reasons for this. For instance, before 1782 it was not legal for Presbyterian ministers to perform marriages, and until 1844 they could not perform 'mixed marriages', i.e. marry a Presbyterian to a member of the Church of Ireland. For this reason many marriages of other denominations, especially those classed as Dissenters, are recorded in the Church of Ireland registers. Marriages between Protestants and Catholics may also be found"*.

The Presbyterian Church

In the 1861 census there were 174,000 Presbyterians in Co. Donegal (11% of the population). This Church was established in Ireland in 1642 at Carrickfergus by Scottish Presbyterians, the so-called 'Scots-Irish', and was further encouraged by plantation landlords such as Sir Arthur Chichester in Co. Donegal. The church was mainly based in Ulster. At the end of the 19th century 96% of all Presbyterians lived in Ulster, mainly in the counties of Antrim and Down. Many Presbyterians had also emigrated to America and played an active role in the American struggle for independence. A full account of the history of the Presbyterian church, and the types and accessibility of their records is given by Christine Kineally in *Irish Church Records* (Flyleaf Press 2001).

There were a number of schisms within the Presbyterian Church in Scotland which also affected the Irish church. In the 19th century a dissenter group known as the Reformed Presbyterians or Covenanters was established and this resulted in more than one Presbyterian church in the same locality. To distinguish these groups, the churches were referred to as 1st and 2nd etc.

Presbyterian Parish Registers

Parish	Bapts	Marrs	Burs	Location
Ballindrait	1819	1845		DAL/PRONI
Ballylennon 1st	1829	1831	1830	DAL/PRONI
Ballylennon 2nd	1845	1845		DAL/PRONI
Ballylennon 3rd	1878			DAL
Ballyshannon	1836	1837		PRONI
Buncrana	1836	1845		PRONI
Burt	1833	1837		DAL/PRONI
Carndonagh	1830	1830		DAL/PRONI
Carnone	1834	1846		PRONI
Carrigart	1844	1844		DAL/PRONI
Convoy	1822	1846		DAL/PRONI
Crossroads	1811	1811		DAL/PRONI
Donegal 1st	1824	1824	1860	DAL/PRONI

Parish	Bapts	Marrs	Burs	Location
Donegal 2nd	1865	1845		DAL/PRONI
Donaghmore	1835	1820	1825	DAL/PRONI
Donaghmore	1834	1846		DAL/PRONI
Drumhome			1845	DAL
Dunfanaghy	1830	1830		DAL/PRONI
Fahan	1899	1845		PRONI
Fannad	1827	1827		DAL
Fannet	1859	1827		PRONI
Gortlee (Reformed)	1872	1872		DAL/PRONI
Greenbank	1862	1864		DAL
Inch	1845			PRONI
Killymarde	1845			PRONI
Kilrnacrenan	1848	1846		DAL/PRONI
Knowhead	1826	1846		PRONI
Letterkenny 1st	1845	1845	1845	DAL/PRONI
Letterkenny 2nd	1821	1821		DAL/PRONI
Letterkenny 3rd	1841	1845		DAL/PRONI
Malin	1845	1845		DAL/PRONI
Milford	1838	1845		DAL/PRONI
Milford (Reformed)	1864	1864		DAL
Monreagh	1845	1860		DAL/PRONI
Moville	1833	1845		DAL/PRONI
New Moville	1865			DAL
Newtown Cunningham	1830	1830	1880	PRONI
NW Donegal Mission	1864			DAL
Pettigo	1844	1846		PRONI
Ramelton 1st	1806	1807		DAL/PRONI
Ramelton 2nd	1808	1808		DAL/PRONI
Ramelton 3rd	1839	1839		DAL/PRONI
Raphoe 1st	1829	1829		DAL
Raphoe 2nd	1860	1860		PRONI
Rathmullan	1854	1845		DAL/PRONI
Ray 1st	1855	1845		PRON1

Parish	Bapts	Marrs	Burs	Location
Ray 2nd	1882	1845		PRONI
St. Johnston	1838	1835		DAL/PRONI
Stranorlar	1821	1846	1831	DAL/PRONI
Trentagh	1836	1830	1843	DAL/PRONI
Urney	1837	1866		DAL

The Methodist Church

John Wesley is credited with founding Methodism and he first came to Ireland in 1747. Methodists existed as a group within the established church until about 1878 when they seperated. Some of the earliest Methodist Circuits had been formed in the north of Ireland after 1818. In 1863 Methodists were first allowed to perform marriage ceremonies in their churches. A full account of the range of Methodist church records, and the types and accessibility of their records is in *Irish Church Records* (Flyleaf Press).

Methodist Parish Registers

Parish	Bapts.	Marrs	Burs	Location
Ardara & Dunkineely	1863	1863	-	DAL
Ballintra	1835		-	DAL
Donegal Mission	1833	1864	-	DAL
Inishowen	1862	1873	-	DAL
Ramelton	1829		-	DAL

Miscellaneous Sources.

In recent years church histories have been published by all denominations to commemorate centenaries, bi-centenaries, etc. Many of these are available in the County Library in Letterkenny. Some are listed in the Bibliography (see p. 135).
 Amongst those of most interest to the genealogist are:

Lecky, Alexander G. *The Laggan and its Presbyterianism*. Belfast; Davidson & McCormack, 1905.
Lecky, Alexander G. *In the days of the Laggan Presbytery*. Belfast; Davidson & McCormack, 1908.

Leslie, James B. *Clogher Clergy and parishes*. Enniskillen: [s.n.] 1929.
Leslie, James B. *Derry Clergy and parishes*. Enniskillen: [s.n.] 1937.
Leslie, James B. *Raphoe Clergy and parishes*. Enniskillen: [s.n.] 1940.
Mullin, T. H. *The Kirk and Lands of Convoy since the Scottish Settlement* (Belfast Newsletter 1960).

EXPLORING IRISH GENEALOGY

No. 1

IRISH METHODISTS - WHERE DO I START ?

Presentation label from " Hammond's March" Sunday School
First Methodist Sunday School in Ireland.

by
Steven C. ffeary-Smyrl *MAPGI*

'Irish Methodists - Where do I start?' by Steven C. ffeary-Smyrl (CIGO 2005)

Abraham Family History. Published privately in U. S. A. Includes church and parish records of Laghey, Drumholm, Taughboyne and Pettigo.
Mevagh Down the Years. Leslie W. Lucas, Belfast 1983. (includes Church of Ireland Clergy, Churchwardens and Presbyterian Clergy from 1776)
More about Mevagh, Dublin 1982. (includes Church of Ireland Clergy 1426-1981, Churchwardens and Presbyterian Clergy from 1840s to 1971)
F*annet (Fanad) Presbyterian Church Index to births and Marriages 1827-1899.* Anne McLaughlin and Brideen Blaney (Pamphlet in DCL).
Richard Hayes. (Ed.) 'Manuscript sources for the History of Irish Civilisation' 11 vols. - Boston, 1965 is a compendium of Irish materials in several international libraries. This contain church related information are:
PRONI D803. Vestry book of Culdaff parish, Co. Donegal, 1693-1804, including entries for Clonea, Co, Donegal, 1693-1707.
NLI MS8130. Petition of parishioners of Donoughmore, Co. Donegal to House of Lords concerning the repeal of the Assumption of Ecclesiastical Titles Act, with 9 pages of signatures, n.d.
PRO M5148. Parochial returns of Finner parish, Co. Donegal. Clogher Diocese, included with Innismacsaint, 1660-1866.
PRONI D10437. Legal and administrative records re. Diocese of Derry and Raphoe, 1746-c.1940, including vestry books for Upper Moville parish, 1773-1899, and for Killaghtee parish, 1782-1872; baptism, marriages and bann entries for Killaghtee parish 1807-1831.

PRONI 999/20. Copy registers of Church of Ireland parish of Killaghtee, baptisms 1810-1830, 1873-1873; banns of marriage, 1809-1814; marriages 1814-1831, and rector's accounts, c.1820.
NAI: Parochial returns of baptisms, marriages and burials made by the incumbent on the occasion of a visitation, for Innismacsaint, Co. Donegal, 1699-1700 and 1811-64.

British Museum: Add Ms. 14,406 (1655-90). Manuscript Map; a terrier to the church land in the parish of Killymard, with a map of part of the parish of Inver and Killymard in the barony of Banagh, Co. Donegal. Certified tracing from the surveys of forfeited lands in British Museum (1655-99).

Chapter 7 Land and Estate Records

Apart from records of land ownership, there are a variety of other land-related records which can be used in family history. Most Donegal people were not land-owners. After the break up of the old Gaelic landholding system at the beginning of the 17th century, the majority of Donegal's population were small tenants on large estates owned by British landlords. The land records of relevance are therefore records which list occupiers of land for purposes of Tax (e.g. Tithe Records, Griffith's Valuation), or records related to land rental (e.g. Estate Records, Land Commission etc). An account of each of these types of records is below.

Estate Records

Estate records are usually a mix of legal papers, correspondence and other material relating to the management of the large estates of land which were common in Ireland until the late 19th century. The administration of these estates produced a large quantity of useful records, including:

o **Leases**: which give the tenants name and sometimes other details. Partnership leases, which were the norm before the break up of the Rundale (locally known as "Squaring of the Land") in the 19th century, will list several tenants.

o **Rent rolls**: showing the rent amount and date of payment. These often do not include information on the smallest tenants, most of whom had no right of tenure, and/or may have been subtenants of the larger tenants or middlemen.

o **Maps:** which may show the holdings of individual tenants

o **Wages books**: in which will be found the names of estate labourers, household servants and gardeners who may not appear as tenants.

25

VALUATION OF TENEMENTS.

PARISH OF CLONMANY.

No. and Letters of Reference to Map.	Townlands and Occupiers.	Immediate Lessors.	Description of Tenement.	Area. A. R. P.	Land. £ s. d.	Buildings. £ s. d.	Total Annual Valuation of Rateable Property. £ s. d.
	CLOONTAGH—con.						
c	Susan M'Loughlin (Owen).		House, office, & land,		1 10 0	0 15 0	2 5 0
d	Rd.M'Loughlin(Dick)		House, office, & land,		1 5 0	0 15 0	2 0 0
e	Cecily M'Gonigle (James).		House, office, & land,		1 10 0	0 15 0	2 5 0
10 f	Dl.M'Gonigle(James), John M'Loughlin,	Ellen M'Clintock,	House, office, & land,	142 1 20	1 10 0	0 15 0	2 5 0
	Edward Tohan(Ard),		House, office, & land,		0 15 0	0 10 0	1 5 0
h	Charles Noone(Ard),		Land,		4 5 0	—	4 5 0
i	Richard M'Loughlin (Dick),		Office and land,		1 10 0	0 10 0	2 0 0
	Charles Doherty;		Land,		0 15 0	—	0 15 0
	Unoccupied,		Land,		0 15 0	—	0 15 0
	Park.Doherty(Anthony)	Same,	House and office,	—	—	0 15 0	0 15 0
11	Park.Doherty(Anthony) & thirty-eight partners	Same,	Mountain,	474 1 20	3 0 0	—	3 0 0
12	John Doherty(Dudley) & fourteen partners	Catherine & Grace Ball and Thomas Torrens,	Mountain,	282 2 10	3 0 0	—	3 0 0
13			Water,	14 2 8	—	—	—
	Total,			1938 3 2	150 15 0	35 15 0	186 10 0
a	ARDAGH. (Ord. S. 3 & 10.) Denis Doherty(Smith)		House, office & land				

Sample entries for the civil parish of Clonmany from Griffith's Primary Valuations (1857)

In conducting a search for Estate records, it is important to establish the identity of the landowner of the estate where the ancestor lived. A useful starting point is Richard J. Hayes' **Manuscript Sources for the History of Irish Civilisation (1965)** commonly known as Hayes' Manuscripts. This work contains more than 300,000 holdings in more than 1,300 archival repositories in 30 countries and is comprehensively indexed. It was compiled in 1965 and also includes sources held in private collections. A supplement covers the period 1965 – 1970.

A related work, **Sources for the History of Irish Civilisation: Articles and Periodicals (1970)** lists 270,000 articles in over 200 journals and periodicals published from 1800 to 1967. These works are on open shelves in NLI, NAI and Dublin City Library and Archive and in several international libraries. It is useful to search these under the heading of 'Rentals: Estate Papers' for Co. Donegal.

Griffith's Primary Valuations (see opposite and P. 62) can also be used to establish the names of landlords, lessors and tenants in the mid 19th century.

Other useful reference sources are :-

Topographical Dictionary of Ireland. Samuel Lewis. London 1837.
Lists the principal proprietors and residents in each civil parish and town.
Land Owners in Ireland: Dublin, 1876.
Lists 32,614 owners of more than 1 acre of land in Ireland in 1876. This information is available on several websites including www. failteromhat.com
The Landlords of Ireland. O.H. Hussey de Burgh 1878.
Lists landlords owning 500 acres or more.
Analecta Hibernica. Nos. 15(1944); 20(1958); 23(1966); 25(1967); 32(1985).
Lists estate records which had been indexed at the date of publication.

Most materials relating to land ownership in Ireland can be found in the NLI, Registry of Deeds, Land Commission and in private collections. The NAI and PRONI also have some material.

The following is a selection of the estate records for Co Donegal, but it is by no means a final or exhaustive list.

Estate Records

Estate	Location	Source	Reference
Arran (Gore Family)	Donegal Town	Lease book	PRONI T3344
		Papers and Accounts	Ms 7585-7/1-203, Ms 7598/1-5, Ms 7617/1-23, Ms 7594/1-32, Ms 7604/1-81, Ms 7623/1-53, Ms 7595/1-8.
Abercorn (Hamilton Family)	Main seat in Tyrone. Co. Donegal, Taughboyne and Raymoghny	1718 Manor Survey	PRONI D/623/Dr/3/1
		Rental and Lettings 1794-1809	D 623/c/4/8
		Lease book 1782	D 623/B/11/1
		Tennant Right Sales from 1800	D 623/B/4
Abraham	Raphoe	1780-1800 Lease	PRONI D/1550/103/1
Alexander	Moville	1737, 1784-89 Leases	PRONI D/2433/A/1/24
Boyd	Ballymacool 19th – 20th Century		DCA P80
Brazier	Ray	Leases 1709	PRONI D78
Cary	Redcastle	1796-1914 Deeds Leases	PRONI D2649/5/1-3 PRONI D2649/5/6
Cochrane	Edenmore Estate	1771-1906 Papers	PRONI T2363

Cochrane continued **Clements Estate**	Clonmany and Redcastle Purchases from Lord Boyne 1743	Tennant List and Maps 1743 Rent Roll	1860-1878 "Mevagh Down the Years" (Leslie Lucas) (p 81-82)
		Maps and Tenants names 1779	"Mevagh Down the Years" (Leslie Lucas) (p 91-92), also NLI 14/ A /17
Connolly	Ballyshannon Estate	List of Tenants 1718	PRONI D 2094/24 A-C
		List of Tenants 1729	PRONI D 2094/33, 34
		Rental 1774, 1782-6, 1800	PRONI T 2825/c/36
	Drumholm	Survey and Tenants List 1770	PRONI MIC/435/20
	Tirhugh (including Trinity College Lands)	Rentals 1718, 1722, 1724-6	PRONI T/2825/C/26
	Castlefinn	Rent Rolls 1707	PRONI T/2825/C/44/1 D/2094/23
		Rent Rolls 1731-4	NLI Ms 17302
		Rent Rolls 1724-1831	NAI Ms 6917/1-19
		Rent Rolls 1772-93	PRONI D2003
Crawford Charley	Ballyshannon Arranmore Bought from Conyngham Estate 1840s	Estate Papers C19 Rentals 1862-85	DCA. T104

53

		Estate Papers	
Conyngham	Main seat Slane Co.Meath Co.Donegal Estates Boylagh, Mountcharles, Rosses, Tyrcallen (Stranorlar)	Rentals and Agents Accounts	NLI Ms 35,392-3
			NLI 35,394-400
		Surveys and Maps	NLI Ms 35,401
		1912 Encumbrances	NLI PC 351
		Estate Papers 1916-1830	PRONI D214
Delap	Ray	Estate Papers 1786-30	PRONI T 1336
		Estate Papers 1773-1894	PRONI D 229 A
Derry (Bishop of)	All Donegal Parishes in Derry Diocese	Rentals 1617, 1688, 1708, 1719	D/683/31, 275, 278, 287
		Lease rents of the see of Derry 1718	D/683/286
		Clonleigh Rental 1790 1767-70 Map and Tenants	PRONI D/2798/3/59 PRONI D/835/1/1-3
Donegall (Marquis of) Chichester Family	Inishowen Estates	Leases 1770-1840	PRONI D2338G:1
		Leases 1840-1868	D652/1236-1480
		Estate Accounts	PRONI T455/1

Family	Place	Records	Reference
Donegall continued			
Doherty	Shaftesbury Papers Inishowen	Estate Accounts	NLI ACC 6009
	Lifford and Buncrana	Rent Roll 1837-51	PRONI D 2958
Erne (Earls of) Crichton Family, Crom Co.Fermanagh	Donegal: Clonleigh Estate	Rentals 1650-1900	PRONI D 1939/1
		Leases 1848-1868	D 1939/8/2
Ferguson	Donagh	Maps and Tenants 1790	NLI Ms 5023
		Names 1838-1842	NLI Ms 8410(2)
		Names 1840	NLI Ms 8410(3)
Folliott	Ballyshannon, sold to Connelly 1718	Rental 1680-87	PRONI T2825/23/1
Forward	All Saints, Burt Portlough	1727 Valuations	NLI Ms 4247
		1782-1786 Major Tenants	NLI Ms 2614
		1790 Rental	NLI Ms 9582
Gage	Castlefinn	1780 Survey and Tenants	NLI ACC 1152
		1840-1844	PRONI D/673/61
Grove	Castlegrove	Estate papers from 1830	NLI m/film 975 also DCA P/88
			TCD V/45
Hamilton	Brownhall (Ballintra)	Estates accounts 1760-1891	R.C.B. Lib MIC 364

Hamilton continued	Ballinamore and Fintown	Estate accounts	PRONI 6926
		Rentals 1818-49	DCA P49
	Castlefinn	Account Book	NAI ACC 1785
		1763-67 Leases	PRONI D/1449/7/1
		1842-1843 Leases	NLI Ms 7938
		1841-1851 Leases	NLI Ms 9737
		1845 Leases	NLI 15B 23;4-5
		1846-1848 Leases	NLI m/f 358
Hart	Clonca, Muff,	1757-67 Leases	NLI Ms 7885
	Kilderry	17- 20th Century Deals	PRONI D30771A & D3077F
		1758-1891	PRONI D2077/A/8
Harvey	Malin	1818-1825 Leases	PRONI D/40/92
	Inishowen	1855 map	PRONI D/40/91
	Clonmany Estate	Estate Papers c1900	DCA P4
	Ballyliffen & Inich	Rentals and	PRONI D3054
	Manager Gweedore Estate	Records1884-7	
Heygate	Castlefinn	1851-1858 Rents	PRONI D673/190-1
Humphrey	Cavanacor	Rentals and Accounts	DCA P25
Irwin	Mucketty, Letter, Kilmacrenan Barony	19th C Rentals	NAI M955
Johnston	Tullybrook (Laghy)	1840-1844, 1855 Rents	PRONI D3805/3/29-41

Name	Place / Description	Document & Dates	Reference
Johnston continued	Stranorlar	Deeds and Paper 1767-1803	NAI ACC 861
		Deeds and Paper 1863-65	NAI ACC 9956
	Derryveagh	Survey & Tenant Names 1833	PRONI D/9956
			NAI M7069
Knox (Of Prehen)	In Co.Donegal:- Moneymore (Ballintra)	Leases 1710	PRONI D80-81
Lecky	Ballinacor	1840-1851	PRONI D2290/1/33-59
Leitrim (Earl of)	Main seat Lough Rynn Co.Leitrim	1846-1908 Rentals	PRONI D1550
	Milford	Estate Papers 1864-66	NLI Ms Collection 81
		Rental 1856	NLI AC 2371
		Rental c1870	NAI Ms 3802
	Manorvaughan		NAI Ms 16,883
	Manorcunningham (Prop. J. Beers)	Report 1857	NAI Ms 7002
Leslie Hill	Main seat Glaslough Co.Monaghan, in Donegal, Pettigo Estate	Rental & Account Books 1682-1940	NAI Ms 19786
Leslie		Valuation 1833	NLI Ms 5813
Londonderry (Lord)	Stewarts of Ballylaun, Newtowncunningham	1833-1856 Rents	PRONI D654/H4/2-14
		1840-1855	D654/R3/72-87

Londonderry (Lord) continued

McCausland	Letterkenny and Stranorlar	1841 Map	D654M2B/1
McClintock	Glenmacquin	1845-1850 Survey	D654/N3A/1-2
Mansfield	Killygordon	1846-1848	D654/N2/24
		1851 Valuation	D654/N1/14-15
		Estate Papers 1860-94	PRONI D669
		1782 Tenants	PRONI D/642/G/9
		Lease relating to Estate 1706-15, 1737-96, 1766-1822	D/1550/78/1-3
Montgomery and	Convoy and Castleogary (Inver)	Rentals 1890s	DCA p 89/4/2
Boytons		Accounts 1920s	DCA p 89/4/3
Murray (of Broughton)	(Later Murray-Stewart Estate)	Rental 1638	Donegal Annual, 54 (2002), pp 61-5.
		Muniment Room, Scone Palace, Perth	
	Balliweell, Duncanally, Killkar and Monorgan	Rent Roll 1673	D/2860/24/1
		Rental n.d. (late 17th C)	D/2860/25/11
		17 Leases 1731	Scottish Record Office GD/10/944
		Survey 1749	NLI 21F66
		1719 Rent Roll	PRONI D/2860/4/25
		1727 Rent Roll	PRONI D/2860/25/10

Murray continued

	1749 Rent Arrears	PRONI D/2860/24/11
	1751 Rent Arrears	PRONI D/2860/12/54-6
	Survey of 1730 & 1775	PRONI D/2860
	1780 Tenant List	PRONI D2860/26/1
	Rent Roll (1775)	PRONI D/2860/16/2
	1842-1843 Accounts	NLI Ms. 5464
Killybegs		
Parishes of Kilcar, Killaghtee, Killybegs Upper and Lower, Killymard and Inniskeel	1842-1845 Rents	NLI Ms. 5465-5470
	1847-1850 Rents	NLI Ms. 5465-5470
	1848-1851 Accounts	NLI Ms. 5471
	1849 Rents	NLI Ms.3084
	1851-1859	NLI Ms. 5472
	1850-1852, 1855	NLI Ms. 5473-5475
	1853	NLI Ms. 5892
	1853-1860	NLI Ms. 4280
	1855-1858	NLI Ms. 5893-5896
Musgrave Estate	Carrick and Glencolmcille bought from Connelly 1868	Townlands Survey 1839	NAI AC1503
Nesbitt	Woodhill Ardara	Tenants	NAI 16M2
	1700-1820 Leases and Papers	PRONI D3045
Raphoe (Bishop)	Rent Book 1674-85	NLI 9987

Estate	Townland/Location	Record	Reference
Stewart	Fannet	1758-74 Rental	PRONI D/2358/4/1
	Ramelton	1785-90 Rental	PRONI D/2358/3/2
	Clondahorky	1813-1853	NAI BR DON 21/1/1-3
	Raymunterdoney, Tullyfern	1832-1904 Rents	PRONI D847/21/C/9
	Dunwiley (Stranorlar)	Estate Papers 1812	NAI 97/32/17
	Knockfair (Stranorlar)	Survey 1812	NAI 97/32/17/2
	Fort Stewart	Estate Papers 1743	PRONI D547
		Rentals	PRONI D859
	Mount Stewart	Survey c1717	NLI 15B16
	Tyrcallen (Stranorlar) sold to Marquis Conyngham 1844	Estate Papers	PRONI D3319
Stewart	Ards (Formerly Wray Estate)	Ards 1810-1925	*???????*
		Tenant Records	NAI ACC 6257
Stubbs	Danby	Account Book 1781-90	PRONI D/2784/5
	Ballyshannon	General Account Books	NAI AC1303
Styles	Kilteevoge	1818-32, 1839-50	NAI MS 3774
	Glenmore	1773 Valuations	NLI Ms.402
		94 Freeholds	PRONI D624
Trinity College Lands	Tirhugh and Kilmacrennan	Rentals and Leases	MSS Dept TCD
		1715 ????????	MUN/P/24
Tredenick (From 1844)	Ardara	Survey 1906-7	NLI 15917
Vereschoyle	Dunkineely	Estate Papers 19th C	RIA (not catalogued)

Wallace	Fahan	Estate Papers 1780 Rents	PRONI D983 NLI Ms.9582
Wicklow (Lord Earl Howard)	All Saints, Burt, Raymoghy		
	Taughboyne	Estate Papers 1601-1973	NLI Ms. Collection 69
Young	Culdaff	1600-1970 Deeds/Leases	PRONI D/3045
Unnamed	Inishkeel	Tenants Lists c.1860 1842-1843	NLI MS 17,722 NLI Ms.7938 also PRONI D3045
Miscellaneous	Labourers cottages	Rental Books 20th C	DCA LAB

Griffith's Valuation

Under the Tenement Act of 1842, a national system of land taxation was introduced. This was based on an estimation of the value of the land or property of each owner. To establish the name of the taxpayer and the valuation of their holdings, a survey of all landholders was conducted from the 1840s to 1860s. This 'Primary Valuation of Tenements' was supervised by Richard Griffiths and is usually referred to as 'Griffith's Valuation'. It records the occupiers of land within each townland, and detailed information on their holdings including the immediate lessor (i.e landlord or middleman) acreage, quality of land, valuation, and OS map reference.

Changes in tenants or lessors which occurred after this Primary Valuation were recorded by the Valuation Office and can be accessed at their office (See p. 146). As all properties are included, it also records churches, schools, graveyards, barracks, corn mills, forges, inns and shops. These details were recorded in Tenure, House and Field Books used by the surveyors who carried out the task. Tenure Books are the most useful as they note the tenant's annual rent and lease duration.

An all Ireland 'Index of Surnames' in the Valuation and the Tithe Books (see below) was compiled in the 1960s by the National Library. The index is useful in that it enables a search for a particular surname to be narrowed down within a county to a specific parish. This Index is available in the NLI and NAI and on microfiche in county libraries and other repositories (see p. 65). Indexes to the entire Valuation are also available on CD from several publishers, and on subscription websites.

Tithes

A Tithe (meaning one-tenth) is historically a church tax. When Henry II convened the Synod of Cashel in 1172 he ordered that tithes be paid on cattle and corn. Until then it is doubtful if payment of tithes was a religious or legal obligation in Ireland. The church in Ireland had a different system of support for the clergy and the writs of Henry II did not apply in west Ulster until after the Treaty of Mellifont (1603). The clergy of the Established Church thereafter got part of their income from Tithes. As all people were legally members of the church, everybody was obliged to pay tithes. Apart from the grievance felt by non-members who had to pay, there was disquiet among members of the church about the way the tithes were levied. Tithes were levied on grain crops and hay but pasture or grazing was exempt from the tithe, which favoured the better off.

In 1823 the Composition Act specified that tithes should henceforth be paid in cash. A further change was that tithe on pasture land had now to be paid. It was then necessary to carry out a valuation of the whole country to determine how much each landholder should pay. A **Tithe Applotment** survey was accordingly carried out by local surveyors from 1823-37. The surveyors assessed the average income that could be expected from each piece of land in each townland.

The results were compiled into parish **Tithe Applotment Books**, listing the landholders and the tithe payable by cash. These books are not a comprehensive survey of householders as they do not include those who lived in towns, landless labourers or those who were exempt. They are, however, the first register of landholders in Ireland. They provide information about the type and amount of land occupied by your ancestors. The Tithe Books are also valuable as a resource from a period when few other records survive.

Tithe Applotment Books for Co. Donegal are in the NAI and PRONI (mf MIC/442) and in Donegal County Library. They are also available on the web on several sites.

Registry of Deeds
A deed is a written legal document by which some person (or group of persons) confers rights in a property or some other legal or equitable right, title or claim to one or more other persons. The majority deal with land tranfers. The Registry of Deeds (www.landregistry.ie) was established in 1708 and from that date no deed was legal unless it was registered at this office. Deeds can be useful in finding information on the middle and upper classes of society, but rarely involve the lower classes. Deeds can be found using a 'Names Index' (but note they are only indexed by grantor and not grantee) and a 'Land Index' (by barony and townland). The reference numbers in the indexes can be used to locate the relevant volume and thus a transcript of the abstract.

Encumbered Estate Records
During the mid to late 19th century, many estates became bankrupt and were sold by public auction to pay off debts. The Encumbered Estates Act of 1849 facilitated the process by the establishment of

an Encumbered Estates Court. In the 1849-1857 period about 3,000 estates were sold. Surviving records, available in the NLI and NAI, include publicity bills, which included details of the estates often with lists of the principal tenants and the basis of their leases.

Irish Land Commission
The Land Commission (ILC) was established in 1881 with the purpose of defining fair rents when disputes occurred between landlords and tenants. It also made loans to tenants who wanted to improve or purchase their land. The ILC needed to be satisfied that a tenant's land could be improved and that a tenant was financially able to repay a loan. To this end inspectors were appointed to visit properties to ascertain these matters. This information is contained within the 'Inspector's Records.'

Edward Keane of the NLI researched material for 9,343 estates and compiled a card index (available on open access at the NLI). It comprises of (1) 'Topographical index' by county, barony and vendor's name. (2) 'Name Index' by vendor's name, estate location and estate number. Using the estate number a description of the estate documents can be found in bound volumes. The most useful genealogical information is the tenant rental lists.

The ILC is in the same building as the NAI but an appointment must be made to access the records. Below is an example of an LC record in the NLI.:

Index	Card Ref	Landlord/Estate	Guide to Material in Box
Vol LC	Box 560	George Miller Harvey Inishowen West & East	Deed Sir Arthur Chichester to Richard O'Dougherty 1610 Rory O'Doughertie to John Harvey 1696. Deeds 1769-1890.Rentals 1872 & 1889.

Congested Districts Board
The Land Act of 1891 established a Congested Districts Board (CDB) to assist areas of particular poverty, including parts of Co. Donegal. The CDB was responsible for the redistribution of land and the relocation

of tenants. It also developed local industries, agriculture and fisheries. The Reports of the Congested Districts Board contain accounts of the work of CDB including reference to persons assisted etc. Copies of these reports are in the NLI and in other libraries.

			Barony
Grier	G6		Raphoe Sth.
Grier	G3		Tirhugh
Grierson		T	Banagh
Grieve		T	Raphoe Nth.
Griffin	G16	T	Kilmacrenan
Griffin	G		Inishowen W.
Griffin	G4		Boylagh
Griffin	G		Raphoe Nth.
Griffin	G4	T	Raphoe Sth.
Griffin	G32		Banagh
Griffin	G2		Tirhugh
Griffith		T	Kilmacrenan
Griffith	G	T	Boylagh
Griffith	G16	T	Raphoe Sth.
Griffith	G2	T	Banagh
Griffith	G9		Tirhugh
Grily		T	Raphoe Sth.
Grime	G		Tirhugh
Grimes	G	T	Inishowen W.
Grimes	G		Raphoe Nth.
Grimes	G2		Raphoe Sth.
Grimes		T	Banagh
Grimes	G12	T	Tirhugh
Grogan	G←		Tirhugh
Grouty	G		Inishowen W.

St. Connell's R.C. Church.

I.H.S.

Memento Mori

Here lie the remains of | William Molloy who
dept | this life May 11th 1855 | aged 71 years

'Altar Tomb' :—

I.H.S.

Erected to the memory of | Michael Bradden | who
departed this life | 4th March 1861 aged 70 | years

Sacred to the memory of | Thomas Arthur
O'Donnell Moore | Inspecting Chief Officer of |
Coast Guards He died April 26th 1855 aged 56 |
and Thomas Arthur O'Donnell Moore | his son
who died September | 12th aged 19 years

'Altar Tomb' :—

I.H.S.

Sacred to the memory of | John Coane | who dept
this life the | . . . day of March 1859 | aged 57
years

'Flat Stone' :—

Here lie the remains | of Teague Brislin | who
departed this life | May 11th 1847 aged | 61 years
Also his | beloved wife Anne | who departed this
life | May 19th 1856 aged 61 years

Requiscat in Pace

Sample page from
***The Journal of the Association for the Preservation of the
Memorials of the Dead - St. Connel's R.C. Church***

Chapter 8 Gravestone Inscriptions

Inscriptions on gravestone or on other memorials within churches (e.g. on windows or pews) can be a very useful source of information on dates of death, and ages, and also on family relationships. In rural areas it was common practice for generations of the same family to be buried in the same plot in the graveyard. Very often information on several generations may be found on one gravestone. However, gravestones cost money, and poorer families often could not afford them. In addition, depending on the types of stone used for the gravestones, they may have weathered so as to obscure the names carved on them. Despite these potential difficulties, they are well worth a search.

Note also that, although no gravestone may mark the resting place, a record of the burial may exist in a burial register of the church or graveyard. Catholic graveyards were technically not legal until the early 19th century, and churches may not have burial registers until the 20th century. An account of the complicated history of denominational graveyards is given in *Irish Church Records* (Flyleaf Press 2001).

Gravestone inscriptions for many graveyards have now been transcribed and indexed and thus a lot of time and effort can be saved which would have been spent visiting the graveyards in person. The transcribed gravestones are available in a variety of sources, particularly local history journals.

There are three major sources of gravestone inscriptions for Donegal:

1. **The Journal of the Association for the Preservation of the Memorials of the Dead** (JAPMD) was published in the period 1888-1937 and included indexes and transcriptions sent in by groups and individuals from all parts of the country. It contains gravestone Inscriptions, and often background information on the families concerned. The contributions vary from single inscriptions to whole graveyards. The contributions tend to cover Church of Ireland graveyards; but other denominations may also be included. (see Illustration on opposite page).

2. The collection at the **Donegal County Library** (DCL) which includes transcriptions made by local groups and also copies of transcription in other libraries.

3. Transcriptions in the series 'Donegal Graveyards' by Eileen Hewson published by **Kabristan Archives** in 2008. This 7-part series (noted as KA in the list below) provides details of approx 6,676 Donegal memorials (mostly pre-1940) and includes some of the material from the above sources, and also new transcriptions made by the author. They are available from the publishers at www. kabristan.org.uk.

McGOVERN

Returned to his native land lieth all that was mortal of
LIEUTENANT TAFFE McGOVERN, late of Northumberland Regiment
of the Fencible Infantry. He fell in a duel on the 2nd March
1802, in the 23rd year of his age.
If the esteem and regard of his brother officers who have
erected this stone to the memory could assist his soul in
its flight to heaven, its ascent must have been rapid and
its reception good.

Inscription from St. Anne's Graveyard, Ballyshnnon,
published in the Donegal Graveyard series by the Kabristan Archives.

The availability of transcriptions from all of the above sources are indicated in the Table that follows. Donegal Ancestry Ltd (DAL) will conduct a search on your behalf (see p. 149) of the transcriptions available to them. Some of the above material, and occasionally new transcriptions, are also made available on the web by local groups and enthusiasts. For instance, some may be found at http://freepages. genealogy.rootsweb.ancestry.com. It is always worth searching the web using the name of the area and search terms such as 'gravestone' and/or 'inscriptions'

If you intend to visit graveyards, note that some are in isolated locations, particularly those attached to old monastic sites. If the present parish church gravestones appear fairly recent and the dates are relatively recent, it is worth establishing if an older graveyard exists elsewhere in the parish.

Finally, abstracts from memorial inscriptions within church buildings in the Raphoe Diocese in Donegal are listed in 'Living stones: a historical survey of the churches of the Dioceses of Derry and Raphoe' by Canon D. W. T. Crooks. St Johnstone, 2001 (ISBN 0-9541540-0-2).

Co. Donegal Gravestone Inscriptions in various Sources

Graveyard	Source
Aghanunshin	DAL, DCL
Ardara	KA Part 7
Ardmore	JAPMD (V)2, 1902; KA Part 7
Assaroe Abbey (Ballyshannon)	Don. Ann. 1957
Balleighan	DAL, DCL, KA Part 3
Ballymore Church of Ireland	KA Part 5
Ballyshannon, St. Anne's	DAL, Don.Ann. 1978; KA Part 3
Ballyshannon (Kilbarron church)	JAPMD 1(1) 1890
Ballyshannon RC Abbey	KA Part 1
Bruckless RC	DAL, DCL; KA Part 6
Burt	KA Part 1
Finner (Bundoran)	JAPMD 1(1) 1891
Carndonagh	JAPMD (VI)1, 1904; KA Part 3
Carne (Pettigo)	DAL, Don.Ann.1989; KA Part 6
Castlefinn (Kilmonaster)	KA Part 3
Castlefinn Church of Ireland	KA Part 4
Clonca	JAPMD (IV) 1, 1898
Clondahorky	JAPMD (V) 3, 1903
Clonmany (Ch. of Ireland)	Dun Laoghaire Gen. Journal (Summer 1993)
Clonmany	JAPMD (V) 1, 1901
Clonmany, Greenbank Presbyterian Church.	KA Part 2
Cockhill	JAPMD (VI)3
SS Conal and Joseph	IGRS (GO)
Conwall	Headstone pictures and inscriptions. DCL
Cooly	JAPMD (V)2, 1902; KA Part 7
Creeslough RC Cemetery	KA Part 4
Culdaff Church of Ireland	KA Part 1
Donaghmore	JAPMD 1(1) 1891

Graveyard	Source
Drumnasillagh	JAPMD (VI)3
Dunkineely Church of Ireland	KA Part 5
Finner	In 'Where Erne and Drowes Meet the Sea' by Rev. P.O.O'Gallachair, 1961; JAPMD 1(1) 1891
Finner Graveyard	KA Part 2
Gartan	DAL, DCL; JAPMD (VI)2
Gartan Churchtown	KA Part 4
Greenbank Presbyterian Church.	KA Part 2
Greencastle Church of Ireland	KA Part 2
Inver	DAL, IGRS (GO); KA Part 6
Inver Old	DAL, DCL; JAPMD (IV) 1; KA Part 6
Kilbarron	JAPMD 1(1) 1891
Killaghtee	DAL, IGRS (GO), DCL
Killaghtee Old	DAL, DCL
Killybegs	DAL, IGRS (GO); KA Part 4
Killybegs St Colomb's Church	KA Part 4
Killydonnell	DAL
Kilmacrenan	DAL, DCL
Kilmacrenan Old Protestant Church and Friary.	KA Part 1
Kilmacrenan Presbyterian & Church of Ireland	KA Part 6
Kilmonaster (Clonleigh)	DAL, DCL
Kilmonaster Castlefinn	KA part 3
Lagg	JAPMD (IV)1, 1898; KA Part 7
Leck	DCL; KA Part 4
Letterkenny (3 graveyards)	KA Part 4
Lifford Old Graveyard.	KA Part 4
Lifford Church of Ireland (2)	KA Part 5
Magheragallon	Irish Family History Vol. 5, 1989; DCL, KA Part 6

Graveyard	Source
Mail	JAPMD (IV)1, 1898
Malin Church of Ireland	KA Part 3
Malin Presbyterian Church	KA Part 5
Moville	JAPMD (IV)1, 1898
Moville Church of Ireland	KA Part 2
Pettigo (see Carne and Templecarne)	
Pettigo (Muckross)	KA Part 7
Raphoe	JAPMD 1(1) 1891
Raphoe Cathedral Church; Bishop's Palace	KA Part 7
Ramelton Church of Ireland	KA Part 3
Ramelton	KA Part 7
Ramochy or Raymochy	DAL, DCL; JAPMD 1(1) 1891
Rossnakill Church of Ireland	KA Part 7
Taughboyne	KA Part 7
Teightunny	KA Part 1
Templecarne CoI (Pettigo)	KA Part 6
Tullaghobegley	DAL, DCL, KA Part 5 & 6
Tullyaughnish	DAL, DCL

Carndonagh Churchyard.

[From the late Dr. R. S. Young, Culdaff House, 1898.]

(Continued from p. 174, Vol. V.)

Died on the 11th of Feb 1791 Captain Robert Carey of the Royal Marines aged 50 years He was generous and humane a distinguished soldier and an honest man.

———

Here lyeth the body of Owen Doherty who departed this life March the 17th 1754 aged 62.

———

This stone was erected by Edward Carroll Police Constable ; in memory of his wife Margaret Carroll who departed this life the 5th of August 1824 aged 27 years.

———

From the Journal of the Association for the Preservation of the Memorials of the Dead Vol VI (1) 1904

Raphoe Wills, 1684-1858.   157

	Date or Probate.
Barclay, William, Figart	1786
Barkly, James, Figuart	1776
Barnett, George, Letterkenny	1804
,, James, Moorview..	1831
,, John, Drumholin [*bond dated* 1715].. ..	*1713
Barr, William, Knockegarran	1773
Barrett, John (Rev.), Inniskeel Glebe	1846
Baskin, John, Mt. Charles	1784
,, Robert, Mount Charles	1833
,, Thomas, Mt. Charles	1789
Bates, *als.* Nimo, Alison *or* Eleanor, Raphoe	1777
,, David (carpenter), Raphoe	*1771
Batho, Ann, Raphoe	*1753
,, John (gardener), Raphoe	1742
Batsford, Mary, Raphoe	1781
,, William, Raphoe	1781
Beane, William, Carrickbreck	*1719
Beatty, George, Carowkenan	*1704
Bell, Andrew, Letterkenny	1738
,, Isabella, Letterkenny	1748
,, *als.* Patterson, Jane. *See* Patterson.	
,, William, Ballyshannon	1847
Benson, Hill (Rev.), Vicar of Kilcar	1837
,, Paul, Letterkenny	*1784
Best, David, Drim	1707

An extract from 'Irish Wills' - Vol 5. edited by Gertrude Thrift
Published by Phillimore 1920. reprinted in 1997 by the
Genealogical Publishing Company (Baltimore) as part of
a combined publication containing all five volumes.

Chapter 9 Wills and Administrations

A will is a legal expression of a person's wishes in regard to the distribution of their property after their death. As wills often mention many family members, and also properties associated with the family, they can be a very useful source.

The instructions contained within a will cannot legally be acted upon until the will is proved, i.e. until a Court decides that it is valid. This process of legalising a will is known as Probate, and the court is known as the Probate Court. The Probate Court will usually approve the executor nominated to implement the instructions in the will, and make judgements on any disputes which arise. When a person dies intestate (i.e. without making a will) or when a will cannot be executed as specified (e.g. if the nominated executor has also died), the Probate Court will also intervene to ensure a proper distribution of the person's estate. This process, called Administration, is the court's decision as to the distribution of the property of the deceased. Although less useful than wills, these are also useful documents for determining immediate family connections.

Before 1858 the Church of Ireland was responsible for proving wills. In each Church of Ireland diocese there was a Consistorial court, which was responsible for proving the wills of the residents within the diocese. If the resident had property valued over £5 in a second diocese the will had to be proved at the Prerogative Court of the Archbishop of Armagh. One common circumstance where this occurred was when the land-holding of the testator crossed the border of the diocese. Other than those families which had lands bordering two dioceses, wills proved in Prerogative Court tended to be made by the wealthy.

Following disestablishment of the Church of Ireland (see p. 38), the 1857 Probate Act transferred Probate jurisdiction from the Church to a new Probate Court. A Principal Registry was established in Dublin, which also functioned as the new Prerogative Court. Eleven District Registries, taking over the functions of the Consistorial Courts, were located in the rest of the Country. County Donegal was served by the Londonderry District Registry until Independence in 1922 and is now served by the District Court Office in Letterkenny.

THOMPSON Mary.

Effects under £20.

17 September.   Letters of Administration (with the Will annexed) of the Personal estate of Mary Thompson late of Donegal in the County of **Donegal** Widow deceased who died 15 August 1857 at same place were granted at **London-derry** to Hugh Stephens Holmes and John Johnston both of Donegal aforesaid Merchants the Executors of the Will of Samuel Thompson deceased the Residuary Legatee.

A typical entry from the Calendar of Wills - 1858, on open shelf in the National Archives of Ireland

The history of Irish wills has been unfortunate as much of the original will material was stored in the PRO when the building was destroyed in 1922. The bulk of the Prerogative wills, Consistorial Administration Bonds and Will Books were destroyed, although all the indexes were saved.

Understanding the nature of wills and related documents which survive is useful in using these records. There are different types of wills (Consistorial, Prerogative and post-1858 wills; and Administrations) and several different forms of record may have survived (complete wills, abstracts and/or indexes). In addition, the information is available for different areas (usually Dioceses). Finally, different agencies (e.g. Registry of Deeds, Land Commission etc) compiled collections of wills for various legal purposes and their collections are usually accessible.

The major central surviving wills collection is now in the National Archives (see p. 145) and this agency has made extensive efforts since 1922 to locate further wills and copies of wills. The collection is indexed and is continually being supplemented. A CD index of these wills is also available from Eneclann (www.eneclann.ie).

Terms used in reference to Wills and Administrations

Abstract: A summary of a will or administration, usually including the executor's name, value of the estate, and names of beneficiaries.

Administration: The decision of a court on distribution of an estate of an intestate, i.e. a person who had not made a will. Either the Prerogative or Consistorial Court decided on the allocation of the estate and appointed an administrator to execute their decision.

Administrator with will annexed: Where an executor is not named or is unable to serve, the court will appoint an administrator, but specifically to execute the will as otherwise defined.

Administrator: The person appointed by the court to distribute the deceased person's estate when no will had been made. This is normally a relative.

Codicil: An attachment to a will made by a testator which adds to,alters, explains or confirms a will previously made'

Estate: The property of a deceased person.

Executor: The person appointed to implement the Instructions in the will. Usually a family member is nominated by the deceased and approved by the court.

Grant Books: Indexes of 'grants'(i.e. various decisions) made by Probate courts.

Index: Index of wills, usually providing only the forename and surname of the deceased and the address and year of the will or administration.

Intestate: A person who dies without making a will, or the state of not having a will.

Probate: The process by which a court declares the will to be legally binding.

Schedule of Assets: A list of all of the assets of a testator which will be distributed by means of a will

Testator: The person who makes a will.

Material	Period	Location	Comments
Prerogative Wills	1536-1800	NAI (note books) PRONI & GO (sketch pedigrees)	Wm. Betham abstracts Collections include Crosley, Jennings, Thrift, Index and Charitable Donations and Bequests.
Prerogative Administrations	1536-1800	NAI - (note books) PRONI & GO-(sketch pedigrees)	
Prerogative Wills Books	1664-1684 1706-1708 (A-W) 1726-1729 (A-W) 1777 (A-L) 1813 (K-Z) 1834 (A-E)	NAI & PRONI (Index)	Also noted in "A Guide to Copies & Abstracts of Irish Wills" Wallace Clare (1930). Reprinted 1972 by Genealogical Publishing Co. Baltimore
Prerogative Administration Grants	1684-1688 1748-1751 1839	NAI	
Day Books	1784-1788	NAI	

Consistorial Wills (Vol 5)	Derry Diocese 1612-1858 Raphoe Diocese 1684-1858	NAI	Ed. Gertrude Thrift Vol 5. Pub by Phillimore 1920
Consistorial Administration Bonds-Indexes	Derry Diocese 1698-1857 Raphoe Diocese 1684-1858	NAI NAI	PRONI T490
Consistorial Grant Books	1812-1851 Derry and Raphoe Diocese	NAI	Damaged - not for public Viewing
Wills Index District Registry of Londonderry	1858-1899	NAI PRONI (mf 15c)	Extant wills or copies in NAI or PRONI. Consolidated Index 1858-1877 in NAI.
Original Donegal Wills	1900-1921		PRONI
Testamentary Card Index (TCI)		NAI	If a will or copy exists it should be in the NAI - TCI

Books and Articles:

Index to Prerogative Wills of Ireland 1536-1810; Arthur Vicars 1897.

Abstracts of Wills at the Registry of Deeds: Vol 1 (1708-1745) P. Beryl Eustace; Vol 2 (1746-1788) P. Beryl Eustace; and Vol 3 (1785-1832); P. Beryl Eustace & Eileen Ellis. Irish Manuscripts Commission.

Raphoe/Derry Diocese Wills in '300 Years in Inishowen'; Amy Young (NLI ref. Ir 9292y1)

Index to Will Abstracts in the Genealogical Office (see p. 146). in Analecta Hibernica 17; 1949; by P. Beryl Eustace.

The Guide to the Genealogical Office Dublin (Irish Manuscripts Commission, 1998) has an index to 7,500 wills and a list of 822 related manuscripts.

---

110   LANE, PATRICK, Castlefin, parish of Donaghmore, Co. Donegal, innholder. 29 Feb. 1792. Precis ¾ p. 28 April 1792.

To his beloved wife Jane Lane his freehold tenement lands in Knockramer [? Co. Donegal] and all his furniture; five shillings and five pence to all his daughters Elizth. McGlaghlin, Margt. Wallace and Jane Coyle in full of what they might demand as being his children.

Witnesses: Jas. Simms, innkeeper, Joseph Mahon, weaver, both of Castlefinn, and John Sime, Tamnacrum, gent., in said Co. Donegal.

Memorial witnessed by: said John Sime and Peter McDonagh, city of Londonderry, notary public.

447, 171, 289658   Jane Coyle (seal)
daughter, her mark.
Jane Lane also being deceased.
Sworn at Londonderry 16 April 1792.

An abstract of a Will from
'Abstracts of Wills at the Registry of Deeds' Vol. 3
edited by P. Beryl Eustace and Eileen Ellis
Irish Manuscripts Commission

Library Manuscripts and Papers:

Abstracts of Wills of Irish Testators at the Prerogative Court of Canterbury; 1639-1698; NLI ms. 1397

Abstracts of Wills made by Protestant Clergy and their Families (18th century); RCBL

Swanzy Collection of Abstracts from Clogher and Kilmore Will Books, Administrations and Militia Lists. Principal names included are Beatty, Noxon, Armstrong, Young, Veitch, Jackson, Mee, Noble and Fiddes. NAI T1747 (1C-53-16)

Inland Revenue: (Information on wills obtained by Inland Revenue) – Available in NAI.

Indexes to Irish Will Registers; 1828-1879; and Irish Will Registers; 1828-1839 NAI.

Indexes to Irish Administration Registers; 1828-1879; NAI

Irish Administration Registers; 1829-1839; NB. Made by people with property in Ireland and England.

Indexes to Wills in Land Commission (mainly late 19th century); NLI

Leslie Collection; NLI - ref. mf P.799

Ainsley Will Abstracts; GO ref 535 & 631

Wilson Collection of Will Abstracts; NLI. ref mf P.1990

GO MS   11: Ulster Diaries 1800-1837 (Register of Peers, baronets and knights).

GO MS   12: Ulster Diaries 1698-1800 (Register of Peers, baronets and knights).

GO MS   22: Lodge's Memorials and Extracts from the Rolls.

GO MS 289: Fisher – Abstracts of Deeds and Wills

GO MS 290: Fisher – Abstracts of Deeds and Wills

GO MS 429: Eustace Index of Will Abstracts

GO MS 498: Montgomery Pedigree

GO MS 778: Montgomery Pedigree

GO MS 702: Gordon MS (Crossle)

Welply Collection of Will Abstracts; RCBL. Indexed in 'Irish Genealogist' 1985/86

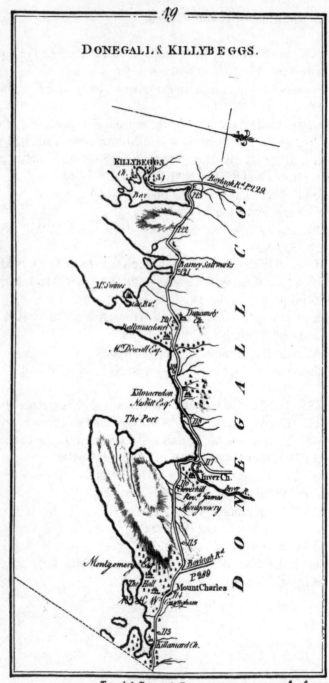

The route from Killybeggs to Killamard from
Taylor and Skinners Maps of Ireland, 1778

Chapter 10 Commercial and Social Directories

Commercial and trade directories were published by private publishers as listings of tradesmen, professionals, clergy and gentry in different areas. Many of them contain other useful local information on the police, militia, court sessions and local administrators. The directories can be useful to both the historian and genealogist alike.

The earliest directories tended to cover only Dublin and its environs but towards the end of the 18th century some publications appeared which give nationwide coverage and can be classed as directory substitutes. These are:

- 1778 – George Taylor and A. Skinners **Road Maps of Ireland** (see opposite page).
- 1783 – The **Post Chaise Companion** through Ireland.

These, as the names imply, were guides for those travelling by coach through the country and list major houses (gentlemen's seats) and their owners as well as the main roads leading from town to town.

Ambrose Leet's Directory was published in 1814. As well as listing gentlemen's seats it noted the nearest town or village as well as the post town nearest the property. Its official title is *A Directory to the Market Towns, Villages, Gentlemen's Seats and other Noted Places in Ireland*.

By the 1820s directories had begun to cover all of Ireland. Pigot & Co's directories (see below) are useful from 1824 and the style and material is augmented both with places and people by Slater's directories and by Thom's Directory from 1845. Many towns and villages of County Donegal are described in detail in both Pigot's and Slater's directories with information describing location, parish, railway stations, churches, constabulary, courts, dispensaries and forts.

Slater's 1870 'Directory of Ireland', for example, listed Bakers, Blacksmiths, Boot & Shoe Makers, Butchers, Butter & Egg Merchants, Carpenters & Cartmakers, China Glass & Earthenware Dealers,

Emigration Agents, Flax & Tow Spinners, Grocers, Hardware-men, Leather Sellers, Linen & Woollen Drapers & Haberdashers, Milliners & Dressmakers, Painters & Glaziers, Physicians & Surgeons, Saddlers & Harness Makers, Seed & Guano Merchants, Shirt Agents, Spirit & Porter Dealers, Tailors, Timber, Coal, Iron & Slate Merchants. Under 'miscellaneous' are found Cornmiller, Whitesmith, Coroner, Straw Bonnet Maker and Dyer & Cleaner. Information on these trades is provided for several towns (see below).

The original copies of these directories are in many libraries including the NLI and PRONI. Pigot's directory (1824) and Slater's directories for 1846, 1856, 1870, 1881 and 1894 are also on microfiche at the National Library and county libraries. They are also widely and freely available on several websites, and copies are available on CD from many sources such as Archive CD Books Ireland

Commercial Directories of relevance to Donegal

1824 Pigot's City of Dublin & Hibernian Provincial Directory:
Covers the towns of Ballybofey, Ballyshannon, Donegal, Letterkenny, Lifford, Pettigo, Raphoe, Stranorlar.

1839 Pigot's City of Dublin & Hibernian Provincial Directory:
Includes the towns of Ballyshannon, Donegal, Stranorlar and Ballybofey.

1839 Directory of Enniskillen, Ballyshannon and Donegal:
lists gentlemen's seats, magistrates, businessmen, Cess Collectors and tradesmen. NLI GO 626.

1846 Slater's National Commercial Directory of Ireland:
Ballyshannon, Bundoran, Buncrana, Donegal, Killybegs and Dunkineely, Letterkenny, Lifford and Castlefin, Moville, Raphoe, Ramelton, Stranorlar and Ballybofey. This edition has almost twice as much detail as its predecessor (published in 1824).

1854 Henderson's Belfast & Province of Ulster Directory:
Ballyshannon and Lifford. Further editions in 1856, 1858, 1861, 1863, 1865, 1868, 1870, 1877, 1880, 1884, 1890, 1894 and 1900.

1856 James Alexander Henderson, The Belfast and Province of Ulster Directory:
Includes an introduction to all nine counties, and a detailed trades directory for every town and village throughout Ulster. There are also a large number of illustrated advertisements which are included.

1856 Slater's Royal National Commercial Directory of Ireland:
Ballyshannon, Bundoran, Buncrana, Donegal, Killybegs and Dunkineely, Letterkenny, Lifford and Castlefin, Moville, Raphoe, Ramelton, Stranorlar and Ballybofey.

1862 Ballyshannon North-Western Directory and General Advertiser:
The First annual issue published at the Herald Office by the proprietor, Andrew Green, 1862. As well as the above, it lists Fair Days. NLI N3613.

1870 Slater's Directory of Ireland:
Ballyshannon, Buncrana and Clonmany, Donegal, Dunfanaghy, Glenties and Ardara, Killybegs, Letterkenny and Manorcunningham, Lifford, Moville, Pettigo, Raphoe and Convoy, Ramelton, and Stranorlar.

1881 Slater's Royal National Commercial Directory of Ireland:
Ballyshannon, Buncrana and Clonmany, Donegal, Dunfanaghy, Glenties and Ardara, Killybegs, Letterkenny and Manorcunningham, Lifford, Moville, Pettigo, Raphoe, Ramelton, Stranorlar and Ballybofey.

1887 Derry Almanac & Directory:
Ardara, Ballintra, Ballybofey, Ballyshannon, Buncrana, Carndonagh, Carrigans, Castlefin, Donegal, Dunfanaghy, Glenties, Killygordon, Letterkenny, Lifford, Manorcunningham, Milford, Mountcharles, Moville, Raphoe, Ramelton, Rathmullan, Stranorlar, and St. Johnston. (Issued annually from 1891).

1894 Slater's Royal National Commercial Directory of Ireland:
overs the same towns as the 1887 edition above.

1824 Pigot's City of Dublin & Hibernian Provincial Directory.
Covers all of the major towns in the county. Available on-line at www.failteromhat.com

1846 Slater's National Commercial Directory of Ireland:
Covers all of the major towns in the county. Available on-line at www.
failteromhat.com

In addition to general directories listing all of the trades etc within towns,
there are also specialist directories or equivalent listing individuals in
particular trades professions or callings:

Directories of Clergy

Clergy are often noted in the above directories, but from the 19th century
the main churches published their own guides.

The Roman Catholic Church has published 'The Catholic Directory,
Almanac and Registry' annually since 1836. This gives a list of priests,
and the locations of parishes and chapels. The 1838 issue contains "the
list of Popish priests that registered at the sessions in 1704". Arranged
by county, it lists the parish, priest, year of ordination, ordaining prelate,
and abode. Other useful Roman Catholic material:
• Maynooth Students and Ordinations, 1795-1895, Hamill, NLI Ir.
  37841 h 15. (Maynooth was the major Irish seminary from 1795).
• Priests Lists (by diocese). 1735-1835, NLI Ms. 1548
• List of Priests and Sureties, 1705, NLI Ms. 5318.

The **Church of Ireland** has published an 'Irish Church Directory'
annually since 1862. Each provides the names of clergy, parishes, etc.
Before 1862 the information available in directories include:
• 'Ecclesiastical Registers' by Samuel P. Lea (1814). Lists
  incumbents only.
• 'Ecclesiastical Registers' 1817, 1818, 1824, 1827 – lists curates as
  well as incumbents.
• 'Ecclesiastical Registers' by John C. Erck (1830) – adds the year of
  the clergy's induction to above.
• The 'Churchman's Almanac and Irish Ecclesiastical Directory' by
  John M. Bourns, (1841).
• 'Irish Ecclesiastical Directory' (1842).
• 'The Irish Clergy List' (1843) also by J. M. Bourns.
• 'Clerical Directory of Ireland' by Sam B. Oldham (1859).
Presbyterian: Information on clergy can be found in:
• McCombs Presbyterian Almanac. NLI Ir 283.

• Names of Presbyterian Clergymen and their congregations in
 Counties Antrim, Armagh, Down, Donegal......, 1837. *New Plan
 for Education in Ireland 1838*, Part I (27-28).

Methodist Clergy.
• Gallagher, W – Preachers of Methodism Belfast. NLI Ms. 287-91.

Legal Directories and Sources.

The admission papers of students to Kings Inns (the centre for
Training of Barristers in Ireland) are the best source for the genealogist
researching ancestors in the legal profession. These include
• King's Inn Admission Papers 1607-1868. (Ed. Edward Keane, P.
 Beryl Phair and Thomas U Sadlier, Irish Manuscripts Commission,
 Dublin 1982). It lists student, fathers name, address, occupation and
 mother's maiden name.
• King's Inn Barristers, 1868-2004. (Ed. Kenneth Ferguson, King's
 Inns 2005)
The original roll/manuscripts date back to 1607 and can be accessed at
the King's Inns Library.

At local level collections of solicitors papers are useful for the
family historian. The NAI in Dublin has papers of Sweeney and Reid
Ballyshannon (not catalogued). PRONI has records of the solicitor firm
of Wilson and Simms of Strabane, Co. Tyrone and Donegal (PRONI
D2609)

Army Records

Many Donegal men served in the British Army and information on
them is available as follows:-
• British Army Records (i) War Office records at the National Archives,
 Kew; Regimental Records; Muster Rolls, Casualties; Widows; Soldiers'
 Documents (pensioners); Registers of Royal Hospital, Kilmainham
 and Chelsea Hospital (Royal Hospital Records are also on microfilm
 at National Archives).

• Births, Marriages and Deaths of army personnel, 1796-1880;
 General Register Office, St. Catherine's House, London.

- 'In Search of Army Ancestry' G. Hamilton Edwards, Phillimore 1977.
- The Irish Genealogist 1985 lists Board of Ordnance Employees at their works (upkeep of harbours and forts) in Buncrana and Enniskillen.
- Navy Lists of officers, masters, surgeons, chaplains of navy ships, coast guards and revenue cruisers. NLI No. 35905.
- Naval Records for Genealogists, N. A. M. Rodger, HMSO, 1984.

Police

The Royal Irish Constabulary (RIC) was the police force in Ireland from 1836-1922. Jim Herlihy's works, which include 'The Royal Irish Constabulary: A Short History and Genealogical Guide', Dublin 1997, and 'The Royal Irish Constabulary; A Complete Alphabetical List of Officers and Men, 1816-1922', Dublin, Four Courts Press, 1999, provide comprehensive information on researching the 80,000 members of Ireland's pre-1922 police force.

The General Register of Service lists all who joined the RIC and their age, height, native county, previous occupation, and religion. Only single men could join so the register also lists the date of marriage (and the authority granting permission to marry) and native county of wife (name not given). Transfers, promotions and cautions are also detailed. The original service records of the RIC are housed in the National Archives, Kew, London (Home Office 184 series). These records are also available on microfilm at PRONI, NAI and LDS Libraries.

Information on members of the Garda Siochana, the police force of the Irish Republic formed after Irish Independence in 1922- can be had from the Garda archives at the Garda Headquarters, Phoenix Park, Dublin. http://garda.ie/museum.html

Medical Profession

Specific medical directories only began in the mid 19th century, but earlier commercial directories list doctors either in the general or separate lists. The **Irish Medical Directory**, which is issued annually, began publishing in 1872. The earlier 'Irish Medical Directory' published in 1846 by H. Croly lists medical graduates of the Royal College of Surgeons in Ireland; the Licentiate Apothecaries of Ireland (some without addresses); and certified practitioners of the Lying-in Hospital. There is also a list of dispensaries and their medical officers, arranged by county, and a general register of Medical Practitioners in Ireland, which is arranged by towns under each county.

An 1852 edition of this directory is more comprehensive and gives an obituary list for 1851. It also contains a list of coroners arranged by county. Similar issues of the Medical Directory for Ireland were published in 1853, 1854, 1856, 1857, 1858, 1859 and 1860.

Specific Donegal Medical Records in DCA include the Irish Medical Association (Donegal Brand) minutes 1903-1977. DCA T13. and the District Nursing Associations: Newtowncunningham, Burt and Killea; Fanad, 1931-1974

Local Government Officials and Employees.

From the early 18th century the Grand Jury was the local administrative body. It levied the county cess, its members presided at the assizes and examined bills of indictment relating to criminal cases. The Grand Jury was responsible for the repair of road and bridges and its presentment books contain the names of those responsible for the repairs as well as maintaining prisons and session houses. The Grand Jury Presentment Books also contain the names of the overseers of the work. These records are available in the Donegal County Archives, and other related material is available as follows:

• Grand Jury Presentments, beginning in 1753 (with gaps) DCA
• Grand Jury Presentments, baronies of Boylagh and Banagh, 1772, 1784-87. NLI Ms 12,910 (MIC/352/1).
• Grand Jury Queries, 1772-83, presentments, 1784-98. NLI n.5374, p.5505.
• Grand Jury Book, Kilmacrennan barony, 1772-98. NAI microfilm reel 22-3.
• Extract from the charter of Lifford, 1611 – PRONI D/1939/18/15/1.
• Court and Borough book, 1716-83 – PRONI D/1939/18/6/9.
• Extract from the 'Book containing the records of the Corporation of Lifford' giving details of tenures and rents, 172(?) – PRONI D/1939/18/14/5.
• Letter of 14 June 1748 giving the names of the warden and twelve burgesses of Lifford in 1727 – PRONI D/1939/18/15/9.
• Co. Donegal High Sheriffs 1607-1814. PRONI PRONI T808/14995.
• Further notes on High Sheriffs of County Donegal in Irish Genealogist (6) 1948.

THE MILLERS & THE MILLS of IRELAND of ABOUT 1850

A LIST COMPILED BY

WILLIAM E. HOGG

Millers and Mills

Millers are listed in "Mill Books" in the NAI. In William E. Hogg's *'The Millers and the Mills of Ireland of about 1850'*, Dublin 1997, Donegal is covered in the O.S. Memoirs Section.

Chapter 11 Newspapers

Newspapers can be a valuable source of family information, although browsing through them can be very time consuming as researchers can be easily distracted by interesting news of the day. Newspapers first appeared in Ireland in the seventeenth century, but the first newspaper established in Co. Donegal was the Ballyshannon Herald in 1831, which was both conservative and unionist in outlook. As a counterblast the Liberator was launched in Ballyshannon in 1839 but lasted only a short time. No further newspapers were published in Co. Donegal until 1885 when the Donegal Independent was first issued.

While the Derry newspapers continued to cover the news in Donegal throughout the 19th century, events in the Donegal Bay area were covered by papers published in Enniskillen in Co. Fermanagh. Strabane papers gave some coverage to events in the central part of the county. At the time, newspapers freely copied items from each other. Many of these papers are available at the libraries in Letterkenny, Derry, Enniskillen and Strabane as well as in larger libraries.

Many of the gentry spent part of the year in, or at least visited, Dublin and London and they feature in papers such as:

- Pues Occurences (first published 1703)
- Dublin Evening Post

For genealogical purposes the best 18th century Dublin papers, which may also contain Donegal news, are

- Faulkner's Dublin Journal (1725)
- The Freemans Journal (1763)
- Dublin Hibernian Journal (1771)

The kinds of information which can be found in these papers include advertisments from local tradesmen, and the social engagements, births, marriages and deaths of the gentry. They also published the names of people involved in petitions, political disturbances and in police and court matters, and occasionally lists of voters or freeholders.

For a more comprehensive account of newspapers and their typical content the following two publications may be useful:

The **Waterloo Directory of Irish Newspapers & Periodicals**, 1800-1900. (Ed. John S. North, 1986) provides an alphabetical listing and description of publications in Ireland in all fields including almanacs, postal directories and newspapers. Copies are widely available in libraries or from the publisher www.nwap.on.ca/irish.html. Below is a sample. entry

> *1296*
> *Enniskillen Chronicle and Erne Packet, The.*
> *1¹-, 10 Aug 1808-31 May 1849, then: Fermanagh Mail and Ennixkillen Chronicle, The. 23 Aug 1849-27 Jul 1893. Enniskillen. Prpitr: Humphrey Bevan; T.R.J. Polson. Pub: T.R.J. Polson Humphrey Bevan (1849). Printer: T.R.J. Polson, Humphrey Bevan (1849) 15cm, 62cm, 60cm (1849) 1d; 2d; 4d (1849). Freq: twice weekly (Mon Thu). Illus: b/w. Subjects: newspapers: newspapers, twice weekly: newspapers, Protestant: newspapers, conservative; poetry; literature; meteorology; gardening. Depts: the press, local news and politics, law sessions, letters to editor, markets, advertising, gardener's calendar, poetry, literature, meteorology, foreign intelligence. Colour: Protestant; conservative. Cmnts: circulates through the entire county and partially in Leitrim, Donegal, Cavan, Monaghan and Tyrone. Merge: incorp with Impartial Reporter (c.July 1893). Source: Mitchell (1846); Shelley & Co, Completer Press Directory. Loctn: PRONI (1824 odd nos, 1880); LHL (1817-1823 imp, 1840-1841); SMC (1808-1812, 1814-1826, 1831-1833) Colin No 489- (27 May 1813, 01 Jan 1824-31 May 1849, 23 Aug 1849-14 Nov 1850, 20 Mar 1851-27 July 1893, [1872, 1875, 1880-1885 imp]); NLI (26 Nov 1808, 28 Apr 1810, 03 Oct 1811, 01 Jan 1824-31 May 1849, 05 Jan-30 Apr 1885, 17 Aug-24 Dec 1885, 07 Jan 1886-15 Dec 1892).*

NEWSPLAN. The NEWSPLAN project originated as a co-operative preservation project for newspapers in Ireland and the United Kingdom. The first report for Ireland was published in 1992, and a revised edition in 1998. The Report has been updated again and is now available in database form on the National Library of Ireland website – www.nli. ie. The report was not intended to act a bibliographic resource, but it has come to be widely used. It arranges the titles alphabetically and by county, indicating the location of each title. It is available in most libraries.

Donegal, Derry, Fermanagh and Tyrone Newspapers

Title	Published	Founded	Location
Ballyshannon Herald	Ballyshannon	1831	NLI, BL
The Liberator	Ballyshannon	1839	NLI, BL
Donegal Independent	Ballyshannon	1885	NLI, BL
Donegal Vindicator	Ballyshannon	1906	NLI, BL
Donegal Democrat	Ballyshannon	1919	NLI, BL
Londonderry Journal (continued as **Derry Journal** from 1866)	Derry	1772-1866 1866	NLI, BL NLI, BL
Londonderry Chronicle	Derry	1829 only	NLI, BL
Londonderry Standard (continued as Derry Standard)	Derry	1836-1964	NLI, BL
Londonderry Sentinel continued as	Derry	1829-1974	NLI, BL
Derry Sentinel		1974	NLI
Derry People	Derry	1902	NLI, BL
Enniskillen Gazette & Commercial Advertiser	Enniskillen	1854	---
Fermanagh Chronicle and Erne Packet	Enniskillen	1808	PRONI, LHL
Enniskillen Advertiser and NW Countries Gazette	Enniskillen	1864	PRONI, LHL
Enniskillen Sentinel	Enniskillen	1877	IBL
Enniskillen Watchman, The	Enniskillen	1848	PRONI
Strabane Morning Post	Strabane	1812	BL, LHL
Tyrone Constitution	Dungannon	1844	NLI, BL
Strabane Chronicle	Strabane	1896	NLI BL

See also the NLI collection at www.nli.ie/en/newspapers-publishing-in-ireland.aspx and the British Library collection at www.bl.uk/collections/newspapers.html

Other newspaper sources:

1. National Library Index to the *Freemans Journal* 1763-1771.
2. National Library Index to marriages and deaths in *Pue's Occurrences* and the *Dublin Gazette* 1730-1740 NLI Ms.3197.
3. National Library Computer index to *London Times* to date, which can be used as a guide index to the Irish Times.
4. *Hayes Manuscripts* should be consulted under 'newspapers' for collections compiled by individuals and lodged in various repositories.
5. Linen Hall, Belfast. *Index to Biographical Material in Belfast Newsletter - 1737-1800)*
6. *"The Irish Genealogist"* published extracts of Birth, Marriages and Deaths by year from newspapers such as
    *   Faulkner's Dublin Journal
    *   Pues Occurences
    *   Finns Leinster Journal
    *   Saunders' Newspapers

Always check your local and county library for Local History Files that contain newspaper clippings.

Marriages.

At Ballintra, by the Rev. John Miller, Mr. James Hamilton, of Ballintra, to Miss Thompson, daughter of Mr. George Thompson, of Drumholm.

On the 3d instat, in Bath, Henry Maunsell, Esq. M.D. to Mary, second daughter of the late Charles Colhoun, of Letterkenny, county of Donegal, Esq.

Dec. 9, in the Cathedral of Dromore, by the Rev. Jas. Saurin, Edward Loftus Neynoe, Esq. eldest son of Col. Neynoe, of Castle Neynoe, county of Sligo, to Charlotte Louisa Saurin, youngest daughter of the

A typical extract from
'The Ballyshannon Herald and Donegal Advertiser" of 1832'

Chapter 12 Education Records

The coming of the Reformation to Ireland meant the destruction of the monasteries as centres of learning and a gradual reduction in the power of the Catholic Church. This culminated in the Penal Laws around 1700 which severely restricted Catholic rights, including the rights of Catholic youth to an education. Those that could afford it, were educated overseas in Catholic Spain, France and Italy.

Nevertheless, some religious groups such as the Quakers, and some local philanthropists opened their schools to all denominations. Towards the end of the 18th century the Catholic clergy favoured the 'hedge school' as the usual type of parish school. Though the term 'hedge school' is used the Irish climate would not have been very suitable for education outdoors and most of the schools were conducted in some rude type of shelter such as a barn or vacant cabin.

While banning education run by the Catholic Church, the Established Church and civil authority eventually saw the need to provide its own system of education for the bulk of the population. Initially it sought a non-denominational model based on Joseph Lancaster's ideas and although this was admirable in concept it proved ineffective in practice because of Ireland's sectarian history.

The National School system was established in Ireland in 1831, which predates the English National School system. In 1835 the 'Report of the Commission on Public Instruction' was published and it lists within each parish the names of all the schools functioning, locations, teacher's names, sources of funds, subjects taught and pupil numbers. The report covered 10,000 schools throughout Ireland.

In the period 1832-1870, 2,500 National schools were established in Ulster. The Commissioners from the outset kept strict control on what was being taught and they initially produced a series of textbooks for the schools. From 1871 'payment by results' was introduced for the teachers and this effectively meant the pupils being examined initially in reading, writing and arithmetic and later in other subjects.

The teacher was paid a sum for each subject passed by each pupil. The sum was added to the teacher's basic salary. This system was abolished in 1900 when a new child centred curriculum was introduced. In 1924 the newly created Free State's Department of Education assumed responsibility for the National schools within its borders.

A report from the Commissioners of Ireland Education Enquiry 1826-27 gives a list of schools in Co. Donegal. The report gives the name of the school, parish, townland, religion and names of schoolmasters and schoolmistresses. The report is available from the NLI, DCL in Letterkenny and in other libraries.

The most useful school records to the family historian are the school rolls, registers and report books.

• **School roll books:** Give name, number, class, and date of birth of pupil.

• **Registers:** Give date of entrance of pupil to school, pupils name in full, date of birth and residence, occupation of parent/guardian, and place where pupil last attended school.

• **District Inspector Report Books:** Account of the inspections of schools.

Registers: The Donegal schools records are located in the schools themselves, in the NAI and there is also a large collection in the DCA. Most of the Co. Donegal school records date from the latter half of the 19th century. The schools with the older surviving registers are listed below (b = boys; g = girls).

Donegal National School Pupil Registers (pre 1900)

School	Registers	Location
Ardara (Wood School)		
Ballaghstrang	1871-1906	NAI
Ballyratton/Castlecanny	1872-1855 b	NAI
Ballysaggart	1890-1925	LDS
Carnshanagh	1874-1938g	NAI
Carrowbeg	1874-1940 g	NAI
Casheland	1878-1957 b	NAI
	1874-1961 g	
Castlefinn	1869-1971	DCA
Coolmore(Ballyshannon)	1871-1967	DCA
Croagh	1892-1972	DCA
Cruachan	1872-1966	DCA
Derryhenny	1874-1962	NAI
Derry Loughan	1873-1962 b	NAI
Dore	1883-1941	DCA
Drumoghill	1882-1927	DCA
Ednaharnon	1873-1976	DCA
Ellistrin	1880-1981	DCA
Glenalla	1872-1960 b	NAI
	1881-1953 g	
Glendooen	1878-1976	DCA
Glendowan	1870-1900	DCA
Glenleigham	1870-1974	DCA
Glenmaquin	1872-1993	DCA
Gola Island	1873-1962 b	NAI
Gulladuff(Moville)	1871-1949 g	NAI
Inishkeragh Island	1886-1953 b	NAI
Inishmean Island	1886-1957 b & g	NAI
Kinelargy Robertson	1885-1943 b	NAI
Letterkenny	1860-1976	DCA
Lettermore(Inver)	1873-1967	DCA

School	Registers	Location
Lettermacward (Robertson)	1899-1979	NAI 2001/82
Lifford	1876-1946 b	NAI
	1874-1945 g	
Lissinisk(Convoy)	1865-1963 b	NAI
	1874-1961 g	
Lough Eske	1857-1956 b	NAI
	1867-1951 g	
Mas-an-Eas	1896-1980 b	DCA
Meenatole	1866-1963 b	NAI
	1892-1963 g	
Meenmore	1872-1998	DCA
Narin	1880-1941 b	NAI
Slieve League	1876-1953	NAI
Straleel	1864-1908	NAI
Stranorlar Boys NS	1891	UCD Archives (P14)
Tank	1863-2000	DCA
Three Trees	1872-1939	NAI
Tulloghabegley	1878-1956 b	NAI
Tullybeg	1880-1957 g	NAI

Key : b = boys ; g = girls.

Apart from the schools mentioned above, the Donegal County Archives in Lifford have the registers of the following National Schools (ages 6 to 12 approx): c. 1855-1990s (dates vary). Note that the names of many schools are in Gaelic. They have been listed by town location:

- Ballyshannon: Scoil Michael O'Cleirigh
- Ballyshannon: Scoil Carraig Na hCorna (2) National School
- Ballyshannon: Scoil Bearaic
- Bunbeg: Scoil Phadraig
- Buncrana: Scoil Iosagain National School
- Buncrana: An Coir Ro-Naofa/Sacred Heart Convent School
- Buncrana: Cockhill Boys National School
- Buncrana: Tullydish/Naomh Baoithin National School
- Burtonport: Min Meannaid

- Burtonport: Acres/Na hAcrai/Ailt an Corrain
- Carrick NS
- Castleshanaghan
- Creeslough Ballymore Church of Ireland National School
- Creeslough: Scoil Mhuire
- Creevy
- Donaghmore National School (Liscooley)
- Donegal National School, The Glebe
- Donegal Killymard: Cill na mBaird
- Donegal: Clar Robertson
- Donegal: Tulaig Sneachta
- Donegal Town: Scoil Aod Rua agus Nuala
- Dooey National School
- Doochary National School
- Dungloe National School
- Dunkineely: Calhaim/Ceallseim National School
- Dunkineely National School
- Dunlewy National School
- Fahan: Naomh Mura
- Fahan: Mura Iochtar and Uachtar
- Fahan: Carrowreagh
- Fanad: Caiseal Mhuire National School
- Fanad Ballymichael National School
- Fanad Scoil Bhrid
- Faugher National School
- Fintown: Scoil Cholmcille
- Fintown: Shallogans/ An tSealgain
- Fintown: Beal-An-Ath-Moir
- Fintown: Ceann Garb
- Glassan National School
- Gortnacart, Ardara
- Kildarrach, Dunfanaghy
- Kilmacrennan: Scoil Naomh Fiachra
- Kincasslagh National School
- Letterkenny Ballyraine National School
- Lettermacaward: Mumhaigh/Dumhai
- Lettermacaward National School
- Lurgybrack: Glenmaquin National School
- Mountcharles: Ardbane National School
- Mountcharles: Glencoagh National School
- Mountcharles: Naomh Peadar National School

- Mountcharles: Muintir Naois
- Newtowncunningham National School
- Ramelton: Droimin
- Ramelton: Scoil Mhuire/St. Mary's
- Ramelton: Killycreen/Na Coilleadh Crine
- Ray (Raphoe) National School
- Rutland Island National School
- Stramore National School
- Termon National School
- Thorr, Gweedore

Registers, or copies of registers, in other archives are:

- Keadue: Keadue Education Society school registers. kept by Denis Mulhern 1831-1834. NLI, MS. Mss. 7358-7359.
- Drumduth: Registers of Drumduth School in Killaghtee. Verschoyle Papers in RIA
- Drumglin: Registers of Drumglin School: 1869-1909. NAI DON. 12;
- Stranorlar: Roll book of Stranorlar Male National School, Co. Donegal, 1889-1891. University College Dublin; Archives Department; P14.
- Kinelargy, Report books, roll books, account books and examination roll of Kinnelargy National School, Co. Donegal, 1886-1941. NAI DON. 22.
- Drumgun (near Donegal Town): Register 1835-1923. NAI Donegal 12/1/2.
- Manorvaughan (Fanad): Register 1878-1970. NAI Donegal 25/1/1.
- Lettermacaward Church of Ireland: 1889-1979 NAI DO 82

Published School Histories:

In recent years there has been a trend to publish school histories to commemorate centenaries, school reunions, etc. Some of them only cover recent years but could still be of interest to the family historian as they often give lists, etc from the registers of an older school in the same area. Many of these are compiled by committee and informally published without author, editor or ISBN etc. Schools are usually covered by parish or local histories – (see p. 135)

The following list, which is by no means exhaustive, deals with some recent school histories:

Ballyboes: The Story of Ballyboes School. Brian Ó Canainn (ed.) Donegal, 2007.

Boyagh (Lifford): "Up the Rocks". Edited by Bobby McDaid, Bundoran 2006

St. Maeartan's: "Smaointe" 1979-2004. 2004.

Carradown: Scoil Naomh Garbháin 1930-2005. Ed. Áine Ní Dhuibne, 2005.

Cloughfinn-Lifford: School History. Chairman Patsy Hagan. Information from 1826.

Craigtown: Scoil Colmcille Letterkenny "My Donegal Then and Now", ed. Helena Gallagher. 2006.

Na Doirí Beaga Scoil Mhuire: Reámhrá Seos Ó Duibhir O.S. 1968-1993. 1994.

Donegal Town: Rural Schools "Schools of Yesteryear" Ed. Helen Meehan. Covers schools in Barnesmore, Clar, Copany, Drumnahoul, Leghawney, Lough Eske, Townawilly and Tullynaught.

Drimarone: "Drimarone School Reunion" (Inver Parish). Ed. Peter Campbell. Schools: Ardbane, Drumnaherk, Letterfad and Lettermore. 2003.

Drumcoe (Mountcharles): 1845-1975. Contains register of School from 1867 to 1975. 2006.

Dromore (Killygordon): Reunion 2005.

Illies(Buncrana): 1838- 1997. 1998.

Killycrean (Ramelton): "Of Saints and Scholars" 1860 – 1900. Ed. Deirdre Friel.

Leac Conail (Ardara): 1900 – 1960. Old School records from 1841. 2006.

Luínneach (Gweedore): 1945-1995. Scoil Adhamhnan Naofa. 1996.

Rathmullan: A Century of Schooling in Rathmullan. ed. Mary Bowden, 2002.

Ray: See Raymoghy

Raymoghy: McClintock, May. "The Heart of the Laggan: The History of Raymoghy and Ray National School" Letterkenny: 1991.

Tamney (Fanad): Tamney Robertson NS. Dorothy Borland. First reference to school in area 1664.

Woodland NS (Letterkenny): 1860-1994. Ed. Adrian Gallagher. 1995.

Post Primary Education

Only a very small number of Donegal people received post primary education before the 20th century. The earliest reference to a college in Donegal is in a recommendation from the first Protestant Bishop of Raphoe, Bishop George Montgomery (1604-1611) that a school be established on the site of a Donegal Monastery. This school, established near Donegal, was transferred to Raphoe in 1663 – the beginning of the Royal School.

Canon D. Crooks book "The 1608 Royal School celebrates 400 years of History 1608" (Armagh 2007) contains a bibliography and a list of sources for this school. Also see Lifford Endowed School records in Donegal County Archives.

Some Donegal students attended Portora Enniskillen – see Richard Bennett in the History of the Royal School. Armagh Royal School – see Tom Duncan in above and "The Marachian" – school magazine since the 1880s and Register of Royal School Armagh – May Ferrar., Belfast 1933.

University Education.

Students from Donegal attended Glasgow University from pre-Plantation times. According to the survey of Bishop George Montgomery of Raphoe Diocese (1606) half of the clergy (R.C.) of the diocese had been to Glasgow University. Information on the students can be obtained from Glasgow University – The Matriculation albums of the University of Glasgow from 1728-1858. W. Innes Addison, Glasgow 1933.

Trinity College Dublin was established in 1593 and there was no other university in Ireland until the 1840s. Trinity students were mainly Church of Ireland, but some Roman Catholics also attended. Students from 1637 to 1846 are listed in Alumni Dublinenses – a Register of the Students, Graduates and Provosts of Trinity College in the University of Dublin (Burtchaell & Sadlier: London, 1924). This is also published on CD by Eneclann (www.eneclann.ie).

WARD, WILLIAM, Siz. (Mr Campbell, Raphoe), Feb. 28, 1706–7 aged 19; s. of Thomas, Generosus ; b. Raphoe, Co. Donegal. Sch. 1709. B.A. Vern. 1711. M.A. Vern. 1731.

An entry from Alumni Dublinenses - see paragraph above

Chapter 13 Emigration Records

Emigration loomed large in all strata of Irish society.   While the poor emigrated due to extreme economic necessity, even the gentry and the minor gentry also often emigrated. The sons of the gentry traditionally pursued careers in the army, navy or civil service and legal professions. Opportunities in these fields in Donegal were very limited and often required that they serve abroad.   Many served with the British Army in what was to become the USA, in India, the East India Company and many other farflung outposts of the British Empire. In addition, of course, hundreds of thousands of ordinary farmers and labourers emigrated in search of a better life.

The best study of emigration from Ulster in the eighteen century is R. Dickson's Ulster Emigration to Colonial America, 1718-75 (London 1966). William Roulston in his "Researching Scots-Irish Ancestors" writes: "Records relating to emigration from Ulster prior to 1800 are sparse. Of the tens of thousands who left Ulster for Colonial America in the eighteenth century, information on their movement has survived for only a fraction."

The Centre for Migration Studies was established to study emigration. It is located at the Ulster-America Folk Park near Omagh, Co. Tyrone and has the best collection of material relating to migration from Ireland. Its Irish Emigration Database (IED) is a computerised collection of over 30,000 records drawn from a variety of eighteen and nineteenth century sources, including emigrant letters, newspaper articles, shipping advertisements, and passenger lists. The IED can currently be accessed in the Research Library of the Centre for Migration Studies, at PRONI, and in the Local Studies Department of the Education and Library Boards in Armagh, Ballymena, Ballynahinch, Belfast, Enniskillen, Londonderry and Omagh. The names of many Donegal emigrants can be found especially in the list of ships leaving from Derry.

The Donegal County Library holds a number of published passenger lists (mainly for vessels leaving Derry Port) and of US and Australian immigration lists. The earliest records date from 1735. They include:

• Donegal Passengers on the Assisted Passenger lists from Plymouth, England to Sydney, Australia 1848-1868 compiled by Richard Reid.

• Emigrants from Ireland to America 1735-1743 by Frances McDonnell.

• Passengers from Ireland: lists of passengers arriving at American ports between 1811 and 1817, by Donald M. Schlegel.

• Irish Passenger lists 1847-1871; lists of passengers sailing from Londonderry to America on ships of the late J. & J. Cooke Line and the McCorkell Line, compiled by Brian Mitchell.

• Passenger list of the 'Invercargill' which sailed to New Zealand 1878 (65 passengers from Co. Donegal).

• Immigration of Irish Quakers into Pennsylvania 1682-1750.

• The Famine Immigrants, listing Irish immigrants arriving at the Port of New York [7 volumes] from 1846 to 1851

OF JOHN MCLEER, peddlar, co Donegal, who came to this country 7 years and 7 months ago, having left a wife and 4 children there who have lately emigrated to this country, and are in Minersville Schuylkill co, Pa, with her sisters and brothers in law; when last heard from was in Massachusetts. Left Minersville in Nov. 2 yrs ago, was about 5 feet 9 inches in height, had sandy fair hair between white and red, eyebrows and lashes nearly white and lost 2 front teeth. Information of him will be received by his wife Ellen McLeer, Minersville, Schuylkill co, Pa.

• The Search for Missing Friends: Irish Immigrant advertisements placed in the Boston Pilot [8 volumes] from 1831 to 1920. The notice above, from the Boston Pilot shows the information that may be found.

Chapter 14 Surnames and Family Histories

Surnames were made mandatory by Brian Boru early in the 11th century and it is likely that the custom had become widespread by the end of the 12th century. Previously people were known by their first name followed by the name of an immediate ancestor – father or grandfather. So a man was "mac" (son of) or Ua/O (grandson of) in the paternal line. People belonged to a sept or clan which gave them further identity. Once surnames became fixed the patronymic ceased to refer to the father's Christian name and descendants simply inherited the surname.

Unfortunately, there was no central control on these changes. In Donegal the Clan Dalaigh took the name O'Donnell from their ancestor Donall Mor. About the same time another sept in West Clare took the same name O'Donnell in honour of their illustrious chief Donal. So both had the same surname although they were no blood relation whatsoever.

Many of the Gaelic septs belonged to the Cinel Conall (see Chap. 1). Erenagh septs lived in most parishes as well. From the conversion of the Irish to Christianity in the 5th and 6th centuries coarbs and erenaghs were connected with the Church. The coarb when a cleric was the successor of the church founder – he was the parish priest or rector. The erenagh/herenagh was manager of the church lands and he had to provide for the support of the clergy and upkeep of the church. These positions were hereditary and the same sept often held the office for centuries.

In the 13th century the O'Donnells brought in gallowglasses to help them in their wars and other Ulster chiefs followed their example. The Gallowglasses were Scottish mercenaries – some of Norse and others of Gaelic descent – and were given land as payment for their services. The Gaelic Gallowglasses had names akin to Irish names – Mac Suibhne, MacDonall, etc, although they were not closely related.

At the Plantation of Ulster many new surnames appeared in Donegal, as in all of Ulster. It was now Government policy to introduce English law, custom and language into Ireland. When Gaelic names began to be written down by Rectors (Tithe Lists), landlords and agents (Rent Rolls, etc.) the names took on new forms. Again there was no standard – the form given depended entirely on the scribe. Some were written down phonetically, thus MacSean became McShane while in another area the name was translated directly into English as Johnson. The Irish Mac an Tuile was phonetically written as Tully – other scribes translated it to its closest phonetical equivalent as Flood.

Lesser known names were often subsumed into more widespread ones, for example O'Leineachan is now being replaced by the more widely known Leonard and the local Cunnea or Ó Coinin is gradually being changed to Quinn – a Tyrone name. As example, the name Campbell today covers several names of widely differing origins in Donegal:

1. The Scottish planter name
2. Some MacAilin came as Gallowglasses and they too are now known as Campbell.
3. The Tyrone-Donegal name MacCath Mhaoil is now known as Campbell.
4. The old Gaelic name McCoilin is now anglicized as Campbell.

Immigration and Emigration.

Many of the Scots who came to Ulster after the Plantation did not remain in Ulster but began emigrating to the new world after 1718. This was partly due to the Penal Laws (see Chap. 1) which also applied to Presbyterians. Some Catholics emigrated in those years but the major Catholic emigration began at the time of the great famine (1845-48). Indeed this flow of emigration continued until the 1970s and 1980s. Emigration to England began in earnest after World War II and again continued until the more prosperous 1970s and 1980s. Seasonal emigration to Scotland was a feature of life for those living in the North West of Co. Donegal for over a century.

According to Dr. Ed. McLysaght *"One of the most striking and interesting of the phenomena to be observed in a study of our subject is the tenacity with which families have continued to dwell for centuries, down to the present day, in the very districts where their names originated. This obtains in almost every county in Ireland...*

The extent to which the present day descendants of the old Gaelic families still inhabit the territories occupied by the medieval septs from which they stem is most remarkable."

This proves true in the case of the names Gallagher, McGroarty, etc.

According to Robert E. Matheson's *Special Report on Surnames in Ireland* (see p. 22/23). Gallagher was the 14th most common surname in Ireland and the third in Ulster after another Donegal name, O'Doherty. According to Matheson the names McGeady, McGettigan, McNelis and Peoples were only recorded in Donegal and more than 75% of the families Ferry, McShane, McGeehin, McGinty, McGinley and Marley were in Donegal also.

Another useful guide for those trying to locate the possible home county of an ancestor is the County Surname Index based on Griffiths' "Primary Valuation of Tenements" and on the Tithe Applotement Books (1824-64). These provide information on the distribution of surnames by civil parish.

There have been many changes in prevalence of local surnames in the past decades, partly due to emigration and returning emigrants. Many Donegal girls have married men from other countries abroad and have returned and settled in Donegal since the 1960s. This adds to the variety of surnames, as do the new immigrants that have made Donegal their home since the 1990s. The biggest change of all is that women can and often do, keep their maiden name. Are we going back to the old Irish custom where a girl who married locally was still known by her maiden name for the rest of her life?

Some common Donegal names, with their Gaelic forms where appropriate, and a note on their origin, are below:

Surname	Origin
ANDERSON:	Son of Andrew – Scottish Planter family from the lowlands and the Borders (England and Scotland)
ARMSTRONG:	Scottish Planter family from the Borders.
ATKINSON:	North of England family – came to Donegal via. Fermanagh.

BARR: Scottish Planter family from Ayrshire.

BARRON: (MacBarúin) son of Barron – Branch of the Uí Neill.

BEGLEY: or O'Begley, (Beaglaoich) – little warrior. Gallowglasses associated with McSweeneys.

BEIRNE: or O'Beírne, As well as being found in Connacht and around Donegal Bay the name is sometimes confused with Burns and Byrne. Spelt Birne also.

BONNER: (MacCrainhsigh), Donegal sept. Sometimes translated as Crampsy.

BOYCE: (O Buí or O'Buadhaigh), or the Norman name De Bús.

BOYD: Originally a Gaelic name. Family settled in Butte and came to Donegal via Ards, Co. Down in 17th Century.

BOYLE: or O'Boyle, (O'Baoighill) Belonged to the Cinel Lughaidh. Originally at Cloghineely, later extended southtowards Donegal Bay.

BRADLEY: (O'Brolachain, O'Brallaghan) – belonged to Cinel Eoghan – sept located west of Derry.

BRENNAN: or Brannan, (MacBranain) - Erenagh Sept in Fermanagh now common in Donegal.

BRESLIN: (O'Breslin), Also spelt Brisland, Brislan – Lords of Fanad pre 12th century. Later erenaghs in Inniskeel. Translated sometimes as Bryne/Brice.

BROGAN: (O'Brogáin), Sept of Uí Fiachrach of North Connacht – now common in Donegal.

BUCHANAN: Scottish Planter family from Stirling.

CAMPBELL: MacAílin, Caímpbéal - see p. 104.

CANNON: or O'Cannon, Likely modern version of Ua Canannaín who ruled south Donegal in the 13th Century. Sometimes written Canning after the English name.

CARLIN: (O'Cairealáin): Erenaghs in Clonleigh parish

CARR:	(Mac Giolla Ceanna) – anglicized form of several Gaelic names. Confused with Kerr or Kerrs.
CARY:	Came from Devon.
CASSIDY:	or O'Cassidy, (O'Casaide) - Ollamhs of the Maguires. Post Plantation many came to Donegal.
CLERY, O'CLERY:	(O'Claraigh), Came to Kilbarron from Connacht in the 13ᵗʰ century and became ollamhs to O'Donnells. Often anglicized as Clark, Clarke.
COLHOUN:	(O'Cathluain) – a Breffny name dispersed through Donegal. Also shortened verion of Scottish name Colquhoun.
COLL:	(MacColla) Gallowglasses from Argyllshire.
CONAGHAN:	(MacConacháin) a version of Irish McCunigan – now often written as Cunningham.
COOK:	English name from the plantation.
COULTER:	Planter family from Lanarkshire.
COYLE:	Mac Giolla Comghaill – sometimes anglicized as McCool or McCole. Had land in Meevagh pre-Plantation.
CRAWFORD:	Came at Plantation from Lanarkshire.
CROSSAN:	(Mac an Crosáin) West Ulster sept mainly in Donegal in the 14ᵗʰ century.
CUNNEA:	(O'Coinin) West Ulster/Donegal Sept now being changed to Tyrone name Quinn.
CUNNINGHAM:	MacCunneagain – Version used today for variety of different names.
	(i) Spelt Conyngham – the family came from Ayr at the Plantation
	(ii) Cunningham – Came as Gallowglasses
	(iii) Used today also for native McCunigan
DEENEY:	or DEENY, (O'Duibhne) - sept from Tullygarvan. – see also Peoples
DEEREY:	(O'Doiridh), Erenaghs in Donaghmore.

DEERMOT:	or O'Dooyer, (O'Duibhne, Dhiorma) - Cinel Eoighan family from East Inishowen – now usually written as McDermott.
DEVENY:	(O'Dubhanaigh) Erenaghs in Kilteevogue and Raphoe.
DIVER,	(O'Duibhir/MacDuibhir), Sept mostly found in Donegal
DOHERTY:	(O'Dochartaigh), From Niall Noigiallach and overlords of Inishowen until 1609
DOOGAN:	(O'Dubhchain) Sept from North West Donegal
DORRIAN:	(Maol Doraidh) Modern version of Maol Doraidh (Mulderry) prominent in the south of Donegal until the 13th century. Later erenaghs in Drumholm.
DUNLEVY:	(MacCun Shleibhe), came from east Ulster to Donegal in 12th century. Became physicians to O'Donnells. Also translated as Mac an Ultagh/McNulty and Ultach.
DUFFY:	(O'Dubhthaigh) Erenaghs of both Culdaff and Templecrone parishes for 800 years
DELAP:	(Originally O'Laipin), translated into English as Delap. Sometimes synonym for Scottish name Dunlop.
EARLY:	(O'Maol Mhocheirigh), O'Mulmoghery – Branch of Conel Eoghan erenagh of part of Clonca.
ELLIOTT:	From Scotland via Fermanagh to Donegal.
ELLIS:	An English name.
ERSKINE:	Family name from South West Scotland at the Plantation.
FARREN:	(O'Farachain) Erenaghs in Clonca Parish.
FERGUSON:	From Fergus a Prince of Dalreada who settled in Kintyre. Family returned at Plantation.
FERRY:	(O'Ferraigh) Mostly a Donegal name.
FRIEL:	(O'Frighil), Ernaghs of Kilmacrennan and Termon
FUREY:	(O'Fiodhadhra) A branch of the O'Melaghlins originally a Donegal sept.

GALLAGHER: (O'Gallchobhair) A 'helper of the foreigner' variously written as Gallachair, Gallegar, etc. A Powerful sept of the Cinel Connall – Marshalls of the O'Donnells.

GALLEN: (O'Gaillin) Belonged to the Cinel Conal.
GALLONN: Erenaghs in Urney.

GILLAN: (O'Giollain) Sept of Conel Eoghan.

GILDEA: (MacGiolla Dé) Sometimes spelt Kildea – erenaghs in Drumholm and Killymard.

Gallagher *Ó Gallchobhair*

The Gallaghers, who were one of the principal septs of Donegal, are still very numerous there. They claimed absolute seniority over the Cineal Connail, the royal family of Connall Gulban, son of the great 4th-century King Niall of the Nine Hostages.

A translation from the Irish for their name, gallchobhair (foreign help), was possibly acquired in the three centuries when they were marshalls in the armies of the O Donnells.

Their notabilities in the main were clerical. Six O Gallaghers were Bishop of Raphoe in Donegal.

Redmond O Gallagher, Bishop of Derry, helped the Armada sailors wrecked off Donegal and was executed by the English.

Frank Gallagher, a journalist who fought in the civil war, was the first editor of De Valera's newspaper, the *Irish Press*. Patrick Gallagher of Donegal, known as 'Paddy the Cope', initiated the idea of co-operative farming.

From Ida Grehan's 'Pocket Guide to Irish Family Names'
Appletree Press Belfast 1985

GILLESPIE:	(MacGiolla Easpaig) Erenagh sept in Kilcar and Kilraine.
GORMLEY:	(O'Goirmleadhaigh) Rulers of Raphoe until driven out by O'Donnells in 14th century. Sometimes now known as O'Gorman, Grimes.
GRAHAM:	An Anglo-Norman family who settled in the Scottish Borders – first came to Roscommon, later to Donegal.
GRANT:	(from Norman Fr. 'Great') Norman family who came to Scotland and later Ulster
HAMILTON:	Scottish name – family at Hamilton in Lanarkshire came at Plantation.
HARKIN:	(O'hEarcain) Erenaghs of Clonca parish, Inishowen
HARAGHY:	(O'hEarachaigh) An erenagh sept in East Donegal now anglicized as Harvey, an English name of Bristol origin.
HARLEY:	(O'hEarghaile or O'Tharlaigh) Son of Tarlach.
HAUGHEY:	(O'hEachaigh) A sept that inhabited the Donegal/Fermanagh border.
HEGARTY:	(O'hEigeartaigh) Branch of the Cinel Eoghain settled in Inishowen.
HILLY:	(MacLilidh) Erenagh in Fahan now usually written as Healy.
HENDERSON:	Scottish Planter family from the Borders and Fifeshire.
HERAGHTY:	(O'hOireachtaigh) Sept found in Donegal And Mayo.
HERRON, O'HERON, O'HARRON:	(O'hEaráin) Sept of Cinel Conal moved from East Donegal to Glenfinn after the Plantation. Sometimes used for Haran – a Scottish name.
HONE:	(O'hEoghan) A Fermanagh sept, but sometimes an English name.
HUME:	Scottish Planter family came from the Borders and Berwick. Name also common in Yorkshire.

IRVINE:	Scottish name from Ayr and the Borders.
IRWIN:	Came from Dumfries at the Plantation.
KEENEY:	(O'Ciannaigh), Erenaghs in Killaghtee.
KELLY:	(O'Ceallaigh), Several unrelated septs who took their surname from Christian name Ceallach. Donegal sept moved from East Donegal in Post Plantation times.
KENNY/KEANY:	(O'Cionnaight) Several Donegal names now also spelt as Kinny, Keaney.
KERR:	(Mac Giolla Ceara) May be a variant of Carr (see above) but can also be a Scottish name likely of Viking origin from Norse 'Kjarr'
KERRIGAN:	(O'Ciaragáin) Harpers of the O'Donnells – lived on lands south of the Erne.
KILPATRICK:	Originally Kirkpatrick, a family from Dumfries, but possibly also from the Irish McGiolla Padraig.
KIRK:	Scottish Planter family name from Kirk – Church.
KNOX:	Scottish family from Renfrewshire.
LAFFERTY:	(O'Laithbheartaigh) Mostly from Donegal and Tyrone.
LEONARD:	(O'Linaird) Now form used for Donegal name Leneghan or O'Leneachain.
LOGUE:	(O'Luoghóg, Ó Maolmhaodhóg) Donegal/ Derry name.
LONG:	Scottish family from Dumfries, came during Plantation.
MACKAY/McKEE:	Scottish Planter family name from Ayrshire.
MAHAFFY:	Scottish Gaelic name – family came to Donegal post Plantation. McAfee another version.
MARLEY:	(Ó Mearthaile) Originally an Oriel name – now mostly in Donegal along the Finn.
MAXWELL:	Scottish family from Roxboro and Dumfries area.

MEEHAN: (Ó Miadhacháin)   Several different septs now spell name the same. One came from Ballaghmeehan in Leitrim, the other from South Donegal, originally spelt Meighan.

MILLER: English name from the occupation.

MONTGOMERY: A Norman family who came to England 1066 – later moved to Scotland and to Co. Down in 1604. Later to Donegal.

MOONEY: (Ó Mianaigh)   Kinsmen of Conal Caol of Inniskeel, erenaghs of Shanaghan near Ardara.

MORRISON: (Ó Muirgheasáin) Erenagh in Clonmany. Bryson used as a translation in Donegal.

MOY: (Ó Múighe) A name of a native Donegal sept from Glenswilly area.

MULDERRY: see Dorrian.

MULHERN: (Ó Maolchiarain)

MULHARTAIGH: (Ó Maol Cartaigh) Sept from Kildoney near Ballyshannon – now use McCarthy.

MULLIGAN: (Ó Maolagain) Owned land in Raphoe Barony. Later erenagh in Kilmacrennan.

MURRAY: (Ó Muireadaigh)   Derived from Murcadh, the last chief of Cinel Boghaine in South West Donegal – slain 1035. Also a Scottish name from Wigton.

McATEER: (Mac an tSaoir) Son of the craftsman. An Ulster name now confused with the original Scottish name McIntyre

McBREARTY: (MacBreartaigh) A Donegal name.

McBRIDE: (MacGiollaBhrighde)   Erenaghs   of Raymunterdoney   parish   and   later   of Gweedore

McCAHILL: (MacCathaill) Son of Cathal, now confused with Tyrone names McCaul & McCall.

McCAFFERTY: (MacEachmharcaigh) - Branch of the O'Donnells

McCAFFREY: (MacCafraidgh) Branch of Fermanagh Maguires.

McCARRON: (Mac Cearain) A Donegal sept from the east of the county.

McCLURE: Scottish Planter family from Ayrshire.

McCOLGAN: (MacColgáin) An Inishowen name – erenaghs in Donagh Parish.

McCREADY, McGREADY: (Mac Reada) Erenaghs in Tullaghobegley and Raphoe.

McDAID: or McDevitt, (MacDaidhíd) A leading Sept in Inishowen..

McDYRE, McDWYER: (Mac Duibhir) A Donegal name not the same as O'Dwyer.

McELWEE: (MacGiolla Bhuidhe) Donegal name often translated as McGillway, McKelvey.

McFADDEN: (MacPhaidin) A Donegal sept formerly located in Meevagh.

McGARVEY: (MacGairbheith) Common in North west Donegal.

McGEADY: (MacGeidi) Common in North West Donegal.

McGEE: (MacAodh, O'Mulgee, Maolgaoithe) Erenaghs in Clondahorky.

McGEEHIN: (Mac Gaoithín) Mostly a Donegal name

McGETTIGAN: (Mac Eiteagáin) Tyrone name found mainly in Donegal. Sometimes a synonym of Gettins.

McGILL: (Mac an Goill) An Antrim sept who migrated to South West Donegal.

McGINLEY: (Mac Fhionnghaile) Donegal name often confused with McKinley (a Scottish name)

McGINTY: (MacFhionneachta) Mostly a Donegal name.

McGIRL: (Mac Fhearghail) In Donegal the version of the name often used is McGarrigle.

McGLINCHEY: (MacLoinsigh) Sept from Glenfinn area.

McGLOIN: (Mac Giolla Eoin), Donegal and Tyrone name, McAloon and McLoon most common in Donegal.

McGOWAN: (Mac Gabhann) Erenaghs in Parish of Innismacsaint – sometimes a synonym of McKeown.

McGRATH: (Mac Craith) Erenaghs in Pettigo, Lough Derg area.

McGRANAGHAN: (Mac Beannachain or Mac Grannacháin) Sept in south Donegal area.

McGROARTY: (Mac Robhartaigh) Keepers of the Cathach, sept located in Drumholm and Templemore.

McKAY/MACKAY: A Scottish name from Ayr. Some came as Gallowglasses, some at Plantation.

McLOUGHLIN: (MacLochlainn) A Prominent Inishowen sept.

McMONAGLE: (Mac Maongail) said to be the same as McGonagle and Conwell and McCongail – erenaghs in Killybegs.

McMENAMIN: (Mac Menamin) Sept formerly located in Letterkenny/Stranorlar area, connected with the O'Donnells.

McNELIS: (Mac Niallais) Erenaghs in Glencolmcille.

McRORY/
McGROARY: (Mac Ruairí) Sometimes translates as Rogers/ Rodgers.

NESBITT/NISBIT: A Scottish family who came from Berwick at the Plantation.

O'BRADAN: Old Donegal name – sometimes translated as Fisher and sometimes translated as Salmon.

O'DONNELL: (O'Domhnaill) Branch of the Clann Lughaidh – Rulers in Donegal for four centuries pre 1603.

PEOPLES: A pseudo translation of the Donegal name Deeney (Ó Duibhne or Ó Daoinaigh) which sounds like daoine, the Irish word for 'people'.

PATTON: (Ó Peatain) A Donegal sept from Ballybofey area. And also a Scottish Planter family from Fife

PATTERSON: Scottish family from Galloway.

QUIGLEY: (O'Coigligh) Sept based in Inishowen

QUINN: (Ó Cuinn) A Tyrone name now common in Donegal.

ROARTY: (O'Robhartaigh) Sometimes confused with McGroarty, erenaghs of Tory and Tullaghobegley.

ROBINSON: A English name common in Donegal.

RODDY: (Ó Rodaigh) Erenaghs in St. Johnston.

SCOTT: Scottish name common all over Donegal. Came from the Borders.

SHARKEY: (Ó Searcaigh) Tyrone name now common in Donegal.

SHEERIN: (Ó Sirín) Sept in Clondahorkey in medieval times.

SIMMS: English family. Came Post Plantation to Lifford/Strabane area.

SINCLAIR: A Scottish Planter family from Caithness.

SHIEL: (Ó Siadhail) From a Christian name. Medical family located in North Donegal.

STRAIN: (Ó Sraitheáin) A sept formerly located in North Donegal.

SWEENEY: (Mac Suibhne) A Gaelic sept who migrated to Scotland and returned as Gallowglasses and then became powerful in Donegal.

STUART: Also spelt Stewart – prominent Scottish family that came after the Plantation.

TIERNEY: (Ó Tighearnaigh) A sept of Donegal now scattered and confused with Tiernan.

TIMONEY: (Ó Tiomanaidh) This sept were the cattle drovers for the O'Donnells.

TINNY: (Mac an tSionnagh, McAshinagh) Donegal form of the name usually translated as Fox.

TOLAN/TOLAND: (Ó Tuathalan) Sept connected with the O'Donnells.

TONER: (Ó Tomhrair) Sept of the Conel Eoghan – located along the Foyle near Lifford.

TRAVERS: (Ó Treabhair/Trower) Leitrim and Donegal sept. Now often a synonym of English Trevis.

VANCE:	A Norman family, originally Vaux, who came to England, and later to Scotland and to Ireland in the plantation.
VAUGHAN:	Family from Hereford and Welsh Borders.
WARD:	(Mac an Bhaird) Donegal poets of the O'Donnells. Moved from Tyrhugh to Leitirmacaward afer the Plantation.
WHORISKY:	(Ó'fhuaruisce/Ó'Uaruisce) translated as Waters.
WILSON:	Most common English surname in Ireland.
WRAY/REA:	A Scottish Planter family from Dumfries settled mostly in Donegal and Derry.
YOUNG:	Mostly a Scottish family from the Borders; also a Culdaff family which claimed they came from Devon.

Family Histories

Gaelic society had its 'fili' (learned poets) who would write special tributes to the chieftains and clans. They also could recite from memory long genealogies of these clans and this oral tradition preceded any written genealogies. Monastic scholars later recorded this oral tradition in written form.

Franciscan Friars from the Donegal Abbey (by then banished from the Abbey and writing 'in loco refugil' - "in our place of refuge") completed a literary work in 1636 of Gaelic history and genealogy from extant sources of the time. It was known as the 'Annals of the Four Masters' or the 'Annals and History of the Kingdom of Ireland'.

The first genealogies printed in a commercial context relate to the aristocracy in England and Anglo-Irish families in Ireland. In the Victorian era a series of county histories were produced which included family histories of renowned families including their coats of arms. The Genealogical Office (see p. 146) whose function is still heraldic i.e., granting of coats of arms, did a certain amount of commissioned research into families and thus has a large collection of Irish family histories. It also accepted donated family histories.

The practice of publishing family histories by the general public began in the 19th century and these can be found in various repositories.

The NLI, the LDS centres, Society of Genealogists (London), Linen Hall Library (Belfast), and various heritage centres and family history societies all have collections of published and unpublished family histories.

The following list is of Co. Donegal family histories that appear in printed works. Others will also be found within the repositories mentioned in this book. Most of the information in the following individual family section is taken from:

1. Mac GIOLLA EASPAIG, Fergus 'The Gaelic Families of Donegal' In Nolan, William, Ronanyne, Liam and Dunlevey, Mairead: Donegal History and Society (DHS henceforth) pp 759-838.

2. Genealogical Office – NLI GO (see p. 146).

Abraham: Abraham Family History – Laghey, Drumholm, Templecairn. DCL

Alexander: Ahilly Visitation of Ireland (vol 3) F. A. Crisp (1911)

Anderson: Anderson of Moville. Anderson, Patrick. Bramhill, Cheshire: [published by author]. DCL

Arkwright: The Arkwright family in Ireland. Arkwright, Thomas J and Peter A. Wigan [published by the author] no date.

Babington: The Babingtons, by Helen Meehan, in "Inver Parish in History", 2005.

Baskin: See **Verschoyle**

Bonner: The Bonner Family History, Sue Bonner Thornton. Waco; Texas: Texan Press 1972.
Bonner origins in Directory of Irish Family Research No. 18. 1995.
Clann Chnáimhsigh – a Donegal Sept. Brian Bonner in Don.Ann. 1979.

Boyd: Robert Boyd of Ballymacool, by Alan Roberts & W. S. Ferguson. Donegal Annual, 1990. The Boyd Family of Ballymacool House, by Brian Boyd. No date, 16p.
From Donegal to Blackguards's Corner: A History of the Boyd Family

of Kaikoura Rangiora [published by the author], 1998, 447p, photos.
Boyd & Lockhart of Donegal. Compiled by James W. Devitt, LDS
Library. See also **Verschoyle**

Boyle/O'Boyle: DHS p. 788-791.

Bradley: DHS p. 793-794

Breslin/Boyce: DHS p. 791-793

Brook: Susanna Marie Brook, her Family and Brooks of Lough Eske
Castle. M. Donnelly in Don.Ann. 1989.
NLI GO. Ms178, pp263-71; pedigree of Brooke of Brookesborough,
Co. Fermanagh and of Killydonnell or Brooke Manor, and of Brook Hill,
both in Co. Donegal, of Dublin City, of Colebrooke, Co. Fermanagh,
c1600-1854.

Cairnes: NLI GO. Ms. 170, pp 57-66; A pedigree of Cairnes of
Donoghmore. Co. Donegal c.1600-1826.

Campbell: DHS. P 762-763;   NLI GO. Ms. 113. pp 459-60; pedigree
of Campbell, Barts., .. of Prospect near Ballyshannon and of Carrig
Buoy, Co. Donegal, c.1720-1891.

Carson: NLI GO. Ms. 179, p. 179; pedigree of Carson of Ballyshannon,
c.1700-1856.

Cary: NLI GO. Ms. 171, p. 69; pedigree of Cary of Templemore, Co.
Donegal, 1641-1816.
The Cary Family of Inishowen, Durham NC [published by the
author].

Cassidy: See Verschoyle

Chichester: History of the Chichester Family from A.D. 1086 to 1870.
A. Palmer Bruce, London: Hotten, 1871.

Coane: The Coane Family of Ballyshannon, p.r. Abigail Coane Leibell,
Conn. USA. Photocopy in DCL, Letterkenny.

Colhoun: PRONI. Belfast: T. 1466; emigrant letters from J. Colhoun, Pennsylvania to A. Reed, Leck, Co. Donegal, 1795, with genealogical notes on the Colhoun and Reed families, 1790-1954.

Cochran: PRONI. Belfast: t.2363; Typescript notes on the Cochrane family, Edenmore, Co. Donegal, 1708-c.1811, and on their family estates in Co. Donegal, 1771 – c.1901, with a family pedigree, 1690-1917.

Conneely: Dickson & Conneely Families of Ballyshannon. A.O'Reilly in Don.Ann, 1959.

Cooke: Cooke and Allen Family Letters (Convoy) Photocopies. DCL

Conyngham: NLI – Conyngham Papers. Collection List No. 53, acc no.1539 (mss 35.424-5) Conynghams of Slane and Mountcharles, by Helen Meehan in Don. Ann.1999.

Coulleths: See **Verschoyle**

Cunningham: J. W. Cunningham & Co. Carrick. Enna Mac Cuinneagain, 2000.
NLI ms 34963. Genealogy of the Cunninghams of Castlecooly & Rockfield, Richard Cunningham.

Crawford: The Crawfords of Donegal and How they Came There. Crawford, R. Dublin. 1886. See also **Verschoyle**

Crichton: Crichton; The Pedigree of the Earl of Erne. Steele, John Haughton. Edinburgh: R & R Clarke, 1891.

Creighton: Creightons of Inver and Killaghtee. Felix O'Neill in Don. Ann.1985.

Crockett: Some notes on Crockett Family of Donegal. Belinda Mahaffy; Don. Ann.2004.

Deane: See **Verschoyle**

Deeney: Na Duibhne-Deeney. Dr. B. Deeney in Don.Ann.1981.

Dever: Ballyshannon – Burkes Colonial Gentry.

Dickson: See **Conneely**

Dill: The Dill Worthies. Dill, James, Reid. Draperstown: Moyola Books & Braid Books, 1992.
The Dill Family (correspondence). Dill, John. DCL
The Dills of Fanad by Sam Fleming. Don.Ann.1982.

Dinsmore: From Drumholm, Donegal to Cartwright, Upper Canada: The Dinnsmore-Freeborn-Strong Families. Conn, Nancy H. Toronto, Ontario, 1988.

Diver: The Story of the Diver Family – From Donegal to North Otago. W. Ray Dobson. 1998, The Diver Trust, NZ.

Dobbins: See **Verschoyle**

Downey: A History of the Protestant Families of Counties Sligo, Donegal and Fermanagh. L. C. Downey, 1930.

Duffy: DHS 804-805.

Dunlevy: DHS 770-772; A Genealogical History of the Dunlevy Family. G. D. Kelley, 1901. pt.pr.

Early: DHS 815; A History of the Early Family in America. Early, Samuel S. Albany, NY: [s.n.] 1896.

Edwards: A Genealogy of the Edwards Family of Gortlough, Rathmullan. Co, Donegal and their descendants. Edwards, Belfast 1977.
Recollections of the Edwards Family of Castlehill, Burt. Edwards, John. Londonderry: 1916.

Elder: Deputy Keeper, PRONI Report. 1951-53 (pp 10-108)

Ferguson: PRONI D.2936; Papers of the Ferguson Family of Donegal, Belfast and Newcastle, including diaries of Dr. James Ferguson, c.1850-1960.

Fitzgerald: Ballyshannon. Kildare Journal III.

Fleming: NLI GO. Ms. 178, pp. 15-20. Pedigree of Flemyng of Ramochy, 1600-1809.

Ffolliott: The Ffolliotts of Wardtown Castle. Anthony Begley in Donegal Annual, 1991.
NLI GO. Ms. 172. pp. 121-3 and 131; pedigree of Folliott, Barons Ballyshannon, c 1050-1742.

Friel: NLI GO. Ms.162, pp. 24-25; pedigree of O'Friell of Kilmacrennan, c.1600-1744. DHS 806-808.

Galbraith: NLI GO. Ms 113, pp.257-60; pedigree of Galbraith of Dunduffe Fort and Shanevalley in Co. Donegal and of Derry City. c.1600-1835.

Gallagher: Muintir Gallchobhair. Fr. P O'Gallachair in Don. Ann. 1973. DHS 809-813: Gallagher Family, Liam O'Gallochar (Private) DCL. A Short History of a Notable Irish Family. P. C. Gallagher, London , 1927. Drake Druer & Leaver Ltd.

Gore: Arran Papers, Originals in Trinity College Dublin. Copies in PRONI in Belfast. Papers on the Gore family – Ms. 7600.1-17. Ms. 7614/1-4, Ms. 7624/1-14, Ms. 7625-35.
NLI GO.Ms.170,p.116; pedigree of Gore of Manor Gore, & Viscount Belleisle, c.1690-1789.

Gillespie: DHS p.772-3.

Graham: The Grahams of Drumcavany. Rosemary Graham, 1988, Canada. Graham/Pattersons of Portage, NY. Compiled by Normal Patterson. Pr.pt.

Gormley: DHS 808-808.

Grove: NLI GO.Ms.164,p.222. Pedigree of Grove of Castle Shannon (Castle Grove), c.1700-c.1800.
NLI GO. Ms. 178. pp. 263-4; Descent of Grove of Castle Grove, Co. Donegal, later Brooke, from Brooke of Brooke Hill, Co, Donegal, 1633-c.1800.

Hall: NLI GO. Ms 168, p. 114: pedigree of Hall of Ards and Tully and Barbadoes, c.1700-1810.

Hamilton: NLI GO. Ms 169, p. 129: pedigree of Hamilton of Ballymadonnell, Co. Donegal, c.1720-1821.

NLI GO. Ms. 800, p. 10: Office report and draft pedigrees on Hamilton family of Mount Charles and Ballymadonnell, 1718-1787.
NLI GO. Ms. 165, pp.81-3: pedigree of Hamilton of Killenure, Co. Donegal c.1600-1768.
NLI GO Ms. 170, pp.161-5: pedigree of Hamilton, of Cadzow (now Hamilton) in Co. Lanarkshire and Roxborough. Co. Donegal, 1314-1823.
NLI GO. Ms 800, p.18: Draft pedigrees of Hamilton of Raphoe (1639-1755) and pedigree of Hamilton of Fintragh, Co. Galway, c.1720-1850.
The Hamilton Manuscripts. Hamilton, Sir James. Belfast: Archer & Sons.
Sir Frederick Hamilton [sn.,sl.,] 23p photocopy. DCL
Hamilton, John Stewart, My times and other times. Ballyshannon: Donegal Democrat 1950.
Hamilton, John, Sixty Years' experience as an Irish landlord. Ed. H. C. White. London: Digby, Long [n.d.].

Harkin: DHS 806.

Hart: NLI GO. Ms 182.pp. 293-8: pedigree of Hart of Risby, Suffolk, of Ballyness Manor, Muff and Culmore, of Kilderry and Doe Castle, all in Co. Donegal, c1530-1923.
Hart of Donegal, Henry R. Hart. London: Mitchell Hughes & Clarke, 1907. 158p.
An Irish Family History. Whitton, K.E. [6 volumes (1) Early Harts (20 Harts of Kilderry), (3) Harts of Glenalla (4) Allmans (5) Hamilton and Garstins (6) Youngs of Culdaff. Limited edition, privately printed, 2003.

Harvey: The Harvey Families of Inishowen, Co. Donegal and Maen, Cornwall. Harvey, G. H. Folkstone: F. Weatherhead, 1927. 178p.
NLI GO. Ms 180, pp. 438-53: pedigree of Harvey of Emlagh & Dunmore and Malin Hall, Co. Donegal, of Glendermitt and Molenan in Co. Derry and City of Londonderry, c. 1650-1889.

Hewetson: The Hewetsons of Ballyshannon, Hewetson, John in Journal of the Royal Society of Antiquaries of Ireland. 1910.

Hegarty: The O'Hegartys of Ulster & Kindred Families, Rev.W. Hegarty in Don.Ann.2 (1948).

Holmes: Carnone (Co. Donegal). NLI GO. Ms. 804, p.21: Draft pedigree and notes of family of Holmes of Carnone, Co. Donegal and Victoria, British Columbia, 1724-1909.

PRONI. T.2333: Genealogical notes relating to Holmes family of Castlefin 1654-1923

Hood: See Thomson

Houston: See McTaghlin

Ingram: NLI GO. Ms. 806, p.3: Draft pedigrees of Ingram of Limavady, Co.Londonderry, & Pettigo. Co. Donegal, 1695-1907.

Irwin: The Irwins of Fermanagh and Donegal. Irish Gen.1. (1941)

Kelly: Report on O'Kellys – Clive Evans in Don.Ann. 1985.

Kerr: PRONI T.1187: pedigree of the Kerr family, Ballyshannon. Co. Donegal, 1831-1945.

Kilpatrick: PRONI DK Report 195(1-5)

Kinnear: Genealogists Magazine. Vol. 7, no. 8. December 1936.

Kirk: Letters and family trees from Kirk family of Mountcharles in the U. S. A.
PRONI MIC/1/158.

Knox: NLI GO. Ms. 169 pp.280-9: pedigree of Knox of Lifford, Co. Donegal, c. 1600-1824.
Andrew Knox (Bishop of Raphoe) & his descendants. Londonderry: Hempton & Co. 1892, 34p.

Laird: Laird, Birth Death and Marriage information, Donegal Ireland. Provided by Steve Herkel, DCL.

Law: NLI GO. Ms. 811(10); Draft pedigrees on family of Law of Glenmount, Newtownards, Co. Down, of Ballymore, Letterkenny, Co. Donegal, 1650-1918.

O'Laverty: Seanchas Chlionne Laithbheartaigh (Laverty), James. Belfast: [s.l.,]. 1891. 24p.

Lecky: Donegal.DK/PRONI Report 1951-53 (p.10).

Leslie: NLI GO. Ms. 174, pp.392-3. Pedigree of Leslie of Dinosamount, later Kincraigie, Co. Donegal, c. 1705-1842.

Lloyd: The Lloyds of Rookville and their namesakes of Croghan, Gray (Edward B). (Irish Genealogist, vol. 1, No. 12. Oct 1942).

Mackay: See **Verschoyle**

Mackemie: PRONI. Compiled c.1890. about the Rev. Francis Mackemie of Ramelton, Co. Donegal, who founded the Old Rehoboth Church, Somerset County, Maryland, in 1683.

Marshall: Marshall of Manor Cunninghan. Being notes on descendants of John Marshall, Marshall. G. F. L. [published by the author], 1931.

Miller: Miller Family Scrapbook. Miller, Janet Eileen. [s.l.: published by the author] 81p. illus.
Miller Family Tree (with supporting trees for Montgomerys Hamiltons, Irwins, Townshends, Beresford/Webbs. Miller, Janet E. [published by the author] 22p. photocopy. DCL.

Montgomery: The Montgomery Manuscripts – compiled by W. Montgomery, Edward G. Hill. Belfast 1869.
NLI GO. Ms. 112, p.202: pedigree of Montgomery of Brenter of Bonnyglyn of the Hall, all in Co. Donegal, c.1680-1807.
The Montgomerys, the Sinclairs and Drumbed House – Helen Meehan in Don. Ann. 1992.
Montgomerys of Alamein & Montgomerys of Moville – Helen Meehan in Don. Ann. 1995.
Montgomerys of Croghan and Convoy – Helen Meehan in Don.Ann. 2000.
Montgomery, Brian. A Field Marshall in the Family. London: Constable, 1973.
Meehan, H. in 'Ancestors of Field Marshall Montgomery of Alamein'. North Irish Roots II, 2000.

Morrison: Ó Muirgheaín. DHS 815-16.

McAteer: Mhac an tSaoir: Guide to the sources for researching McAteer families in Ireland. Ed. Shane McAteer & Brian Traynor. Belfast: Ulster History Foundation, 1994. 63p,

McCain: Descendants of John McCain from Stranorlar Parish. Co. Donegal, Ireland. Brian W. Hutchinson, CG, FSA (Scot). Columbia, Canada 2005.

McCailin: MacCailín – a Martial Clan. Brian Bonner in Don. Ann. 1981.

McCausland: Conyngham Papers in NLI. Ms 35, 426. PRONI D669: Macausland (McCausland) family papers, a collection of papers relating to property in Strabane, Co. Tyrone, Stranorlar, Letterkenny, Co. Donegal 1600-1942.

McClintock: NLI GO. Ms 112, 00318-21: Pedigrees of McClintock of Traintaugh, Prospect, Lifford, Dunmore and Taboyne in Co. Donegal c.1630-1791.

McColgan: The McColgans of Inishowen. JRSAI 12 (1871), 23 (1893), 32 (1909)

McCrabb: See **Thomson**

McDermott: see O'**Duibh Dhiorma.**

McDaid/McDevitt: DHS 767-8. MacDaibhéid – Descendants of Pug Nosed Ó Dochartaigh – Brian Bonner in Don.Ann. 1992.
Journey – James and Agnes Leonard McDade Family From Donegal to Scotland to Kansas – Anne McDaid Barrett. DCL

McFeeters: Pedigrees of the McFeeters, Baird and Laird families. Co. Donegal, 1642-1962. PRONI T 2747 (Part):

McGarvey: McGarvie Family History. McGarvie, Michael. [Self Published] 1995, 222p.
Fanad on Foot-Genealogical Explorations in Donegal (McGarvie). Glastonbury: 1989, 62p.

McGeehin: Our Donegal McGeehins 30p. Photocopy. P. Ringel. DCL

McGettigan: Early History of the McGettigan Septs. Dan McGettigan in Don Ann. 1990.

McGrath: Pettigo and its people, including a history of the Clan McGrath. 2002, 112p; ill. John B. Cunningham.

McKinley: Draft pedigrees of McKinley of Ballintra, Co. Donegal, 1752-1876. NLI GO. Ms 819 (14):

McLaughlin: DHS 773-6. The Mac Laughlins of Clann Owen. Brown, John P. Boston: W. J. Schofield, 1879.

McMenamin: Our McMenamin Story (Glen Swilly). B&N.Fitzgerald. P.p in Victoria, Australia.

McMonagle/ McGonigle: DHS 787.

McNaughton: The McNaughton Family of Grange, Burt Parish, Donegal. Edited by Gary Hawbaker. 2006, Hershey, PA, U. S. A.

McTaghlins: McTaghlins & Houstons of Donegal. Joseph Houstons in Don. Ann. 1980.

McSheffrey: McSheffreys of Inishowen. C. E. Swezey in Don Ann. 1978.

Nesbitt/Nisbit: Nesbitt of Woodhill, pedigree in Swanzy Notebooks, RCB Library, Dublin.
History of the Nesbitt or Nisbit Families in Scotland and Ireland. A.Nesbitt. Torquay 1898.
The Nesbitts of Kilmacredon (Inver) – Helen Meehan in "Inver Parish in History".

Newburgh: PRONI. T1183: pedigree of the Newburgh family of Lifford and Castlefin, Co. Donegal and of Ballyhaise, Co. Cavan, c.1650-1900.

O'Cannon: History of the O'Cannons of Tír Chonaill. T. G. Cannon in Don.Ann. 1978.
DHS 794-6.
'Ua Canannáin genealogies in the Irish Manuscript tradition' In Studia Hibernica No. 30, 1998-1999 [published 2000]

O'Cleirigh: DHS 796-804.
O'Cleirigh Family of Tir Chonaill. Walsh, Paul. Dublin: Colm O Lochlainn, 1938, 52p., index.

O'Doherty: DHS 800-804.
O'Doherty People and Places. Ó Dochartaigh, Seoirse F.. Whitegate, Co. Clare, 1998. ill.
Ó Dochartaigh Clan. Origins of the O Dohertys: pedigree and family group sheet. Carndonagh: Inishowen Tourism, 1995. [the Ó Dochartaigh Clan issue regular newsletters and packs on genealogy and Clan history].
Origin and History of the O'Dohertys. Anthony Matthews. Published in Colpe, Drogheda, 1973.
NLI Ms 27,711c. History of the O'Dogherty family of Inishowen and Spain by Ramón Salvador O'Dogherty Sanchez of Spain, 1 vol., nd.

O'Donnell: Ó Cleirighs Life of Red Hugh O'Donnell. Ed. Peter Murphy, Dublin, Fallon 1890.
Clann Dalaigh (O'Donnell). Vincent O'Donnell. Kilmacrennan: O'Donnell Clann Gathering Committee, 1989. 81p. illus. Reprinted and updated 2007.
The O'Donnells of Glashagh, Glenfinn. O'Donnell, Eunan in "Dearcadh" 2007-2008.
NLI GO. Ms. 165, pp201-3: pedigree of O'Donnell of Ballyshannon, Co. Donegal. C. 1603.1772.
NLI GO. Ms 112, pp 238-44: pedigree of O'Donnell, Prince of Tyrconnell, Barons Donegal and Earls of Tirconnell, of Larkfield, Co. Leitrim, of Greyfield in Co. Roscommon, of Caffersconce in Co. Donegal, of Newport and Newcastle and Erris, Co. Mayo and of Austria, c.1400-1811.

Ó Duibh Dhiorma: N. McDermitt, DHS 805-806.
Ó Duidhiorma – Lord of Bredagh. Brian Bonner for Inishowen Development Group, 1987.

O'Laughlin: Families of Co. Donegal. Kansas, USA. 2001.

Ó'Peatain: Notes on O'Peatains of Donegal, Mayo & Roscommon. Ir.Gen. 4(4) (1971):303-07. See also **Patton**

Parke: Genealogy of the Parke Family 1720-1920. John P. Wallace p.p. 1920 (Donegal).

Paterson: Paterson of Plaister & Swillymount in Visitations of Ireland (V2.) F. A. Crisp (1911).
NLI GO Ms 34, 960/1-2 Paterson, John, Dean of Christchurch. 2 Vols on History of Dean John Paterson's family, and connected families, mainly in Co. Donegal.
The Patterson and Pattison Family Association Record Book – 4. Patterson, Norman G. [s.l.:s.n] 1967, 215p.

Patton: 'There is an old house in Ireland': the Patton Family and Croaghan House 1636-1990. Burton, Patricia. DCL. See also **O'Peatain**

Polk: Cavancor House and President Polk's Ancestors. Eddie O'Kane, Don. Ann. 1989.
Pogue/Pollock/ Polk: genealogy as mirrored in history: from Cotland to N. Ireland/Ulster, Ohio and Westward. Welch Pogue, Lloyd. Baltimore MB: 1990.

Porter: The Porters of Bury by Rob Porter. Published by author Minnesota, U. S. A. 1994. See also **Verschoyle**

Rentouls: The Rentouls of Second Ray by a descendant in Don Ann.1979.

Robb: George Robb-Catherine Forsyth and their descendants 1807-1982. Robb, Dale and Arlene. [s.n. s.l.] 1982. 68p. Illinois, U. S. A.

Rogan: Hugh Rogan of Counties Donegal and Sumner: Irish acculturation in frontier Tennessee. Shelley Hankins, Caneta. In Tennessee Hist. Quarterly Vol LIV Winter 1995

Roarty: DHS 816

Shaw: See **Verschoyle**

Shovlin: The Shovlin Family From Ardara 1863-1984. From Shovlin Reunion 1984.

Smyth: NLI GO Acc 3789. Genealogy of Smyths of Carrickaduff, Derrynoose, Carragh Keady. Co. Donegal, 1990.

Stuart/Stewart: Our Line of Stuarts. Martha Stuart Helligos, 1987, Nebraska.

Lt. William Stewart of Cumberland County, Pennsylvania. Rehins, Joe. Published by the author 2005. Traces the life of Stewart family from Ramelton.

Stewarts of Ramelton. Nelson, Peggy. Photocopied items relating to this family. U. S. A. published by the author. Pennsylvania, 2002.

PRONI T1662: pedigree of the Stewart family, Fortstewart, Co. Donegal c.1500-1900.

Pedigree of the Stewarts of Ballylawn, Co. Donegal, now Marquesses of Londonderry (Genealogists Magazine vol. 7, no.10, June 1937).

NLI GO MS. 179 pp.45-8. Pedigree of Stewart of Doone, Kings Co. of Hornhead, Co. Donegal c.1680-1860.

Strong: The Strongs from Donegal. Alec Strong. DCL

NLI GO Ms 114. pp.2-4: pedigree of Stronge, Barts., of Balcaskie, of Strabane and Clonleigh, and of Croghan in Donegal. C.1650-1862.

Stubbs: Visitation of Ireland – F. A. Crisp Vol I.

Swan: NLI GO. Ms. 171 pp.531-2: pedigree of Swan of Buncrana. c.1830-1939.

Sweeney/McSweeney: Clann Suibhne na Midóg. Niall O Domhnaill in Don.Ann. 1948.

Origins of Clann Suibhne. R. Mingo Sweeney in Don.Ann. 1990. DHS 778-788

Fr. Paul Walsh – Leabhar Claínne Suibhne. Dublin, Three Candles 1911.

'The Sweeneys' in The Irish Link No 47, December 1995, p.18.

The Sweeneys: Fanad, Doe, Banagh, international. Ed. John P. Sweeney [Clann Suibhne] 1997.

Sween (Suibhne): Clann of the Battle-axe: a brief history of the Mac Sweeney Gallowglasses. Sweeney, Richard Mingo. Gaoth Dobhair: Clann tSuibhne, 1999.

Daniel McSweeney 1831-1893. Diane Lovegrove Bader. June 22 2003 (Sweeney Doe Clan Reunion)

NLI GO Ms 171 pp.423-30: pedigree of Sweeney (formerly Swyny) of Fanad in Co. Donegal c. 1650-c.1805.

Sinclair: The Montgomerys, the Sinclairs and Drumbeg House. Helen Meehan in Don.Ann. 44 (1992).
Genealogy of the Sinclairs in Ulster. Sir John Sinclair, Dublin 1867.

Stinson: Extracts from records of Drumholm Parish 1695-1900. Stinson, Mowbray, Cockburn, Thompson and Taylor Families. Compiled by D. W. and H. S. Stinson (LDS Library 929 2415 Al No. 28).

Thomson and **Hood**: PRONI T.1264. Pedigree of Thomson & Hood families, Moyle, Co. Donegal from the 17th century; & McCrabb family, Altaghaderry, Co. Donegal, from mid 18th century; summary of the diaries of John J. elder, Ashgrove, Co. Donegal and Toronto, 1881-1898 (photocopies).

Thornley: The Thornleys – Bram Stoker's Donegal Roots. Billy Finn in Don Ann. 2005.

Tredenick: A History of Camlin Castle and the Tredenick. Noel O'Loughlin. Viking Publications, 2007.

Trench: DHS 853.

Vance: Vance Family History: memoir of the Rev. George Vance D.D. Allen, Samuel. Dublin: Hodge Figgis, 1901, 252p.

Vaughan: PRONI T.1567. Pedigree of the Vaughan Family of Buncrana. Co. Donegal c.1600-1763.

Verschoyle: Papers in RIA inc. information for Deane, Dobbins, Coulleths, Mackay, Cassidy, Crawford, Baskin, Porter, Boyd, Shaw and Walker families of Killaghtee.
NLI GO Ms. 180. pp.301-9: pedigree of Verschoyle of Castleshanaghan & Tullydonnel. with descent through Stuart, Lord Ochiltree, and Hamilton, Earls of Arran, from Edward I., King of England and Robert Bruce, King of Scotland, c.1690-1891.

Walker: See **Verschoyle**

Ward: DHS p.763-4.
History of the John Ward family of Ramelton. Bernice Ward, 2000. A. B. Canada.

Warnock: Genealogy of W. Warnock & Mary Wilson of Dunfanaghy 1801-1999 p.p. Ohio by Bruce Warnock.

White: White Family of Lough Eske, White, Henry [s.l., s.n.] 1992, 44p. Visitation of Ireland (Vol 2) F. A. Crisp, 1911.

Wilkinson: NLI GO. Mss 811 (13); Draft pedigree of Wilkinson of Creeslough and Dunfanaghey c.1750-1882.

Wilson: The Wilsons of Upper Cavan (1818-1895), R. A. Blair in Don. Ann. 1991.
Giving Destiny a Hand. T. N. & P. E. Wilson, Mooroopna, Victoria, 1992. See also **Warnock**

Woods: GO Ms. 176 pp.181-90: pedigree of Woods of Trinsallagh, and Dowish and Ballyboe, Co. Donegal. Ontario, c.1600-1907.

Wray: The Wrays of Donegal. C. V. Trench, Oxford 1945, with history of Wray, Donnelley, Johnston, Waller, MacDaniel, Atkinson, Jackson.

Young: 300 years in Inishowen. Young, Amy. Belfast: McCaw, Stevenson & Orr. Linenhall Press 1929. With pedigrees, trees, engraving, portraits, arms of Young, Hart, Harvey, Doherty, Knox, Montgomery, Cary, Davenport, Benson, Vaughan, Latham, MacLaughlin, Hamilton, Skipton, Richardson, Stuart, Gage, Boyd, Crofton, Day, Staveley, Laurence, Homan, ffolliott, Cuff, Synge, Nesbitt, Ball, Chichester, Smith, Ussher, Torrens.
Youngs of NW Ulster or "Tracing the Three Black Piles on a Silver Base". Young, G.
Lough Eske. GO Ms. 171 p.223: pedigree of Young of Lough Eske afterward Brook, c.1740-1830. See also **Hart**

Books that contain several family histories as well as other information

"Killymard Ancient and Modern", edited by Canon H. Trimble and compiled by Margaret Graham. Pub 2002 by author. This book details the history of families based on records of R. W. Mercer, Rector of Killymard (1899-1907) which are kept in the Custody of the late Charles Gold and Margaret Irwin. The families listed are:

The Arnolds
John Barnett Boyd of Ballywheel
The Crommers
The Corrigans
The Crawfords of Killymard
The Ellis Family
The Fawcetts
The Golds
The Grahams
Hamiltons. Orbeg
Hewitts of the Glen
Hewitts in Lacrum
Johnston Family of Killymard
The Hendersons
Hetheringtons the Loves
Mackeys
The Magees
The Monteiths
The Montgomerys
The Mooreheads
Morrows of the Haugh
Isaac O'Donnells Family
The Pearsons
Perrys of Ballywheel
Richie of the Glen
Vances of Edrim Glebe
Scott Family of Killymard
Simms
The Stewarts of Drumgun
Torrens
The Warks of Orbeg
The Williamsons of Killymard
The Wilson of Killymard
The Wrays of Killymard

Arranmore Links – Arranmore Links: the families of Arranmore. Gallagher, Barney. [Dublin: Aiden Gallagher] 1986.

Castle Caldwell – Castle Caldwell and its Families. Cunningham, John B. Enniskillen: Watergate Press, 1980, 209p.

Irish Immigrants in the land of Canaan, Miller, Kerby A., et al. Letters and memoirs from colonial and revolutionary America 1675-1815. Oxford & New York; Oxford UP, 2003. [Correspondents include Alexander Crawford of Drimark, Killymard; James and Hannah Crockett of Killeagh; Rev. Francis Allison, of Leck; and Robert McArthus of Burt].

Ó Domhnaill, Niall. Na Glúanta Rossanacha. B. Á.C.: Oifig an tSolathair, 1952.
Information on O' Donnell, Gallagher, Bonner, Sharkey, Duffy, Ferry, McCailin, Ward and Mac Greana, etc. and other local families.

County Donegal Book of Honour. Letterkenny: County Donegal Book of Honour Committee 2002. 225p; ill. [list with annotations and arranged by town/parish, of persons from County Donegal who were killed in World War I].

CONYNGHAM.

Of the County Donegal.

Crest : A dexter arm in armour vambraced, brandishing a sword ppr.

ALEXANDER CONYNGHAM (or Cunningham), a scion of the House of Glencairn, Scotland, settled in Ireland, *circa* A.D. 1600. Possessing a love of wild and romantic scenery, the lake, the mountain, and the ocean, he resided in Rossgul, in the co. Donegal. Here, with a people, whose language was Gaelic, he determined to pass the residue of his life; and here in a castle once dwelt MacSweeney, the Milesian chief of that district, but who was then the tenant of a neighbouring cabin, whilst the solitary Castle reminded him of the former wealth and power of his ancestors. The chief was beloved by the people : they saw in him the representative of an illustrious family, and paid him respect and reverence accordingly. Alexander Conyngham married his daughter. Sometimes ascending, with his son-in-law, the summit of lofty Mackish, the Chief would point out the immense territory of which he had been deprived by the "Plantation of Ulster," observing : "That Castle now deserted and covered with ivy will endure for ages, and oft recall the days of other years, while I, the last of its Chiefs, shall sleep in the tomb of my fathers."

The entry for Conyngham from
'Irish Pedigrees on the Origins and Stem of the Irish Nation'
by John O'Hart (Dublin 1892)

Boards of Guardians

There were 8 Boards of Guardians in Donegal, covering the Poor Law Unions of Ballyshannon, Donegal, Dunfanaghy, Glenties, Inishowen, Letterkenny, Milford and Stranorlar. Parts of the east of the County were included in Derry and Strabane Unions, but their records are not held in Lifford. The Minute Books of the Boards run to over 100 ft. and they date from the 1840's to 1923. As well as the Minute Books the following may be of use in genealogical research:

Punishment Book 1879 – c. 1900: 165 entries giving name, offence and punishment: no details of location.

Separate register (September 1913 – March 1922) giving full name, address, age, occupation and religion for individuals admitted to or discharged from the Fever Hospital or Infirmary of Glenties Poor Law Union.

Outdoor Relief, Admission and Discharge Book (1908 – 11), probably Inishowen PLU, including name of person, or head of family relieved and amount of relief allowed.

Workhouse Admission Register, December 1850 – October 1866) Glenties PLU: 4,960 names giving age, occupation, religion, location, date of admission and discharge.

Indoor Relief Register (1856 – 1915) probably for Dunfanaghy PLU: 5,000 names with age, address, religion, occupation and date of discharge or death.

Milford Workhouse Indoor Register (1880 – 97) (BG119/G/3): 5,000 names.

Donegal Union Indoor Admission and Discharge Book (1919 – 21).

Ballyshannon Clothing Receipt Book (April 1905 – September 1924).

Glenties Indoor Relief Register (1914 – 1921).

Inishowen Workhouse Admission Register (September 1849 – May 1859) (BG97/G/2): 5,000 names. At the back of the book there are lists of orphans and deserted children hired out of the Workhouse (May 1853 and 1 January 1857 – 1 January 1858), noting name, person to whom hired and employment (mainly herding cattle).

Indoor Relief Register (March 1914 – September 1924) possibly for Donegal PLU.

Dispensary Committee Minute Book (March 1852 – 1899) Stranorlar PLU.

Report Book of Visiting Committee of Milford Union Workhouse (6 April 1846 – 25 May 1912).

Minute Book of Co. Donegal Branch of Irish Medical Association 1903 – 1977.

Grand Jury Public Orders (1831) with manuscript annotations.

Letterkenny Workhouse Admission Register (1864 – 77) (BG109/E/1): 4,120 names.

Workhouse Admission Register (1907 – 11) Inishowen (?) Workhouse (BG97/G/6): 5,000 names.

Indoor Relief Register (1907) Glenties: 5,140 names.

Indoor Relief Register (1899 – 1907) Inishowen (BG97/G/5): 5,000 names.

Abstract from 'North Irish Roots' Vol.2 (5) 1990
showing some of the local government documents held in the Donegal Archives collection (see p. 149).

Chapter 15 Bibliography

There are 3500 titles of Donegal interest in the Donegal County Library (DCL) in Letterkenny (see p. 149). It would not be possible to list them all here. The following are some of those of particular interest to the family historian. The major journals publishing articles on Donegal can be found at the end of this chapter.

The following list is divided into two sections:

A. Related to the county as a whole – the titles give background on history, archeology, folklife and churches with the genealogist in mind.

B. Related to specific areas or parishes. Beginning at the Leitrim border on the Drowes the list covers areas in a northward direction around the coast to Innishowen and then south along the Foyle to the Finn.

Published Works

A. Books related to the county as a whole

Donegal – History and Society. Edited W. Nolan, L. Ronayne and M. Dunlevy. Geography Publications Dublin 1995.

Ó Cléirigh, Michael (Annála Rioghachta Eireann) Annals of the Kingdom of Ireland, by the Four Masters, from the earliest period to the year 1616. Edited by John O'Donovan. 7 vols, Dublin: Hodges, Smith 1856,

O'Donovan, John. Letters containing information relative to the antiquities of the county of Donegal collected during the process of the Ordnance Survey in 1835. Lifford [S.N.] 1946.
Ordnance Survey Memoirs of Ireland. Vol. 38. Parishes of Donegal I 1833-5; north Donegal. Edited by Angélique Day and Patrick McWilliams. Belfast: Institute of Irish Studies, QUB, 1997.

Ordnance Survey Memoirs of Ireland. Vol. 39. Parishes of Donegal II 1835-6; mid west and south Donegal. Edited by Angélique Day and Patrick McWilliams. Belfast: Institute of Irish Studies, QUB, 1997.

Archaeological Survey of County Donegal; a description of the field antiquities of the county from the Mesolithic Period to the 17th Century A.D. Brian Lacey et al. Lifford: Donegal County Council 1983.

The Civil Survey A.D. 1643-1656. Counties of Donegal, Londonderry and Tyrone vol. III. Prepared by Robert C. Simington. Dublin: Stationery Office 1937.

Doherty, William James. Inis-Owen and Tirconnell: being some account of antiquities and writers of the county of Donegal. Dublin: Traynor, 1895.

Murphy, Desmond. Derry, Donegal and Modern Ulster, 1790-1921. Derry: Aileach Press, 1981.

Rowan, Alistair. North West Ulster. Harmonsworth: Penguin 1979 [The Buildings of Ireland].

Meehan, C. P. The Fate and Fortunes of Hugh O'Neill, earl of Tyrone and Rory O'Donnell. Earl of Tyrconnell; their flight from Ireland and death in exile. Dublin: Derry 1870.

Ó Cianán, Tadhg. The flight of the Earls. Edited by Paul Walsh. Dublin: McGill, 1916.

Micks, William L. An account of the Congested Districts Board for Ireland. Dublin: Eason & Son 1925.

Maguire, Edward. A history of the Diocese of Raphoe. Dublin, 1920 in 2 vols.

Mullen, E. J. Mount Silver looks down (a supplement to Maguire's History of Raphoe). Glenties: Quinn, 1952.
Gebbie, J. H. and others. In his hand 1870-1970. (s.l.) Universal 1970 (history of C of I parishes, Derry and Raphoe Diocese).

Leslie, James B. Clogher clergy and parishes. Enniskillen: [s.n.] 1929; Derry clergy and parishes. Enniskillen: [s.n.] 1937; Raphoe clergy and parishes. Enniskillen: [s.n.] 1940

Lecky, Alexander G. The Laggan and its Presbyterianism. Belfast: Davidson & McCormack, 1905; In the days of the Laggan Presbytery. Belfast: Davidson & McCormack, 1908

Bayne, S. G. On an Irish Jaunting-Car Through Donegal and Connemara. Harper, 1902.

Gwynn, S. Highways and Byways in Donegal and Antrim. Macmillan, 1899.

Doyle, J. B. Tours in Ulster; a handbook to the antiquities and scenery of the North of Ireland. Davidson.

Doherty, William James. Inishowen and Tirconnel. Traynor, 1859.

Tuke, James H. A Visit to Donegal and Connaught. London : Ridgeway, 1880.

O'Hanrahan, Brenda. Donegal Authors, a Bibliography. Irish Academic Press, 1982.

Dorian, Hugh. The Outer edge of Ulster; a memoir of social life in nineteenth century Donegal. Edited by Breandán Mac Suibhne and David Dickson. Dublin: Lilliput Press, in association with Donegal County Council, 2000 [the manuscript memoir of Hugh Dorian, one-time schoolmaster in Fanad].

B. Books related to specific areas or parishes

Ardara: McGill, Lochlann. In Conall's footsteps. Dingle: Brandon Press, 1992.
McGill, P. J. History of the Parish of Ardara. Donegal Democrat, 1970.

Ballybofey: Ballybofey and Stranorlar Parish Roots by Noel Farrell (Longford 1996) - Includes listing of: 1901 and 1911 Census; Griffith's Valuation (1858); Slater's Street Directory (1894).

Ballyshannon: Maguire, Edwd. Ballyshannon, Past and Present. Bundoran Stepless [193-]

Allingham, Hugh. Ballyshannon: Its History and Antiquities [Ballyshannon: printed by Donegal Democrat] 1937.

Barron, Edward. Ballyshannon, the rare old times [Ballyshannon: printed by Donegal Democrat] 1989.

Ballyshannon Family Roots by Noel Farrell (Longford 1996), Includes listing of: 1901 and 1911 Census; Griffith's Valuation (1858); Slater's Street Directory (1894).

Bundoran: O'Gallachair, P. Where Erne and Drowes Meet the Sea; fragments from a Patrician Parish [Ballyshannon, printed by Donegal Democrat], 1961.

Carrick: Mac Cuinneagáin, Conall. Glencolumbkille, a parish history. Dublin: Four Masters Press 2002, 327p.

Cloughaneely: McLaughlin, Gerry. Cloughaneely: Myth and Fact. An Fál Carrach: the author, 2002. 304p

Derryveagh: Vaughan, W. E. Sin, sheep and Scotsmen: John George Adair and the Derryveagh, 1861. Belfast: Appletree Press, 1983.

McClintock, May. After the battering ram: the trail of the dispossessed from Derryveagh, 1861. Letterkenny: An Taisce, 1991.

Donegal Town: Donegal Town, Inver and Mountcharles Family Roots by Noel Farrell (Longford 1997)

Includes listing of: 1901 and 1911 Census; Griffith's Valuation (1858); Slater's Street Directory (1894).

Donegal Town: Sweeney, Malachy. The Sands of Time – History of Donegal Town and its environs. Tir Hugh Press, Donegal, 2006.

Garrigle, Joe. Donegal profiles [Ballyshannon: Donegal Democrat] [198-]

Drumholm: Egan, Bernard. Drumholm [Ballyshannon: Donegal Democrat] 1986.

Hamilton, J. S. My Times and Other Times. Donegal Democrat n.d.

Hamilton, John. Sixty Years of experience as an Irish Landlord. Memoirs of John Hamilton of St. Ernan's Donegal.

James, D. John Hamilton of Donegal – this Recklessly Generous Landlord. Draperstown, 1998.

Fanad: Fitzgerald, John and John McCreadie. Glenvar and Oughterlin. Carndonagh: Foyle Press [198-]

Glencolumbcille: Herity, Michael, Gleanncholmcille; a guide to 5,000 years of history in stone. Dublin: John Augustine Press, 1971.
Manning, Aidan, Glencolumbkille 3000 BC-1985 AD [Ballyshannon: Printed by Donegal Democrat] 1985. see also **'In Through'**

Glenfinn: MacMenamin, Liam. Glennfinn [n.d.]

Glenties: Briody, Liam. Glenties and Inniskeel [Ballyshannon: Printed by Donegal Democrat] 1986.

Gweebarra, Beyond the: Harkin, William. Scenery and antiquities of north-west Donegal. Londonderry: Irvine, 1893.
McDevitt, James. The Donegal Highlands. Dublin: Murray, 1865.
Swan, Henry Percival. Highlights of the Donegal Highlands. Belfast: Carter: 1955.

Gweedore: Hill, George, Facts from Gweedore. London: Hatchards. 1887.
Hill, George, Facts from Gweedore with Useful Hints to Donegal Tourists. Dublin: Phillip Dixon, Handy, 1845.
Ac Fhionnlaoich, Seán. Scéal Ghaoth Dobhair. B.A.C.: Foilseacháin Náisiunta, 1983.
Ó Gallachobhair, Prionnsias. History of landlordism in Donegal. Ballyshannon: Printed by Donegal Democrat, 1962.

'In Through': (Local name for parishes of Kilcar & Glencolumbcille).
Stephens, James. Illustrated handbook of the scenery and antiquities of south western Donegal. Dublin: McGlashan & McGill, 1872.
Kinnfaela: T. C. McGinley. The cliff scenery of South Western Donegal, embracing detailed notices of St. John's Point, Killybegs, Sliabh Liag, and Glen-Head. Londonderry: Journal 1867. Re-printed 2000 by Four Masters Press, Dublin [with an introduction by Michael Herity and biographical note by Éanna Mac Cuinneagáin].

Innishowen: Swan, Harry Percival. Twixt Foyle and Swilly. Dublin: Hodges Figgis.
Bonner, Brian. Our Inis Eoghain heritage. B.A. C.: Foilseacháin Náisiúnta, 1974.
Harkin, Michael (i.e. Maghtochair). Inishowen: its history, traditions and antiquities. Derry: [printed by the Journal] 1867.

Swan, Harry Percival. The Book of Inishowen. Buncrana: Doherty 1938.
O'Carroll D. The Guns of Dunree, 1986.
Bonner, Brian. Where Aileach Guards B.A.C.: Foilseacháin Náisiúnta, 1974.
Campbell, D., Dowds, D & Mullan, D. Against the Grain – Burt and its People 2000.
McGlinchey, Charles. The last of the name. Belfast: Blackstaff. 1986.
Harkin, Maura and McCaroll, Sheila. Carndonagh [s.l. s.n.]. 1984.
Beattie, Sean. The book of Inistrahull. Carndonagh: Lighthouse, 1992.
McLaughlin, J. A. Carrowmenagh, History of a Donegal Village and Townland. Letterkenny, 2001.

Inver: Meehan, Helen. Inver Parish in History. Donegal: The Author, 2005. See also **Donegal Town**

Islands: Gallagher, Barney. Arranmore links [s.l.: s.n.] 1986.
Duffy, Margaret. Inishfree: a tribute to Donegal island and its people. [Letterkenny: printed by Browne Printers] 2004.
Fox, Robin, The Tory islanders: a people of the Celtic fringe. Cambridge: Cambridge UP, 1978.
Aalen, F. H. and H. Brody. Gola: The life and last days of an island community. Cork: Mercier Press, 1969.

Kilcar: O'Donnell, Michael. By the Kilcar Hearth. Ballyshannon:1987.
O'Donnell, Michael. 'In-through' people. Letterkenny: Printed by Donegal Printing] 1946. 154p; ill. see also **'In Through'**

Killaghtee: McGill, P. J., History of Parish of Killaghtee. Donegal Democrat, 1968.
Byrne, Packie, M. Recollections of a Donegal Man. Compiled and edited by Stephen Jones. Millinghton, 1989 1st.

Killybegs: Conaghan, Charles. History and antiquities of Killybegs, Ballyshannon [printed by Donegal Democrat, 1975].
Conaghan, Pat. Bygones: New Horizons on the history of Killybegs [s.l.: s.n.], 1989.

Killymard: Trimble, Harry. Killymard: Ancient and Modern. Donegal Town. The Author, 2002.

Kilmacrennan: Strain, Hugh. In Kilmacrennan Long Ago. [Letterkenny: printed by Browne] 1997. 128 p. ill.

The Laggan: Campbell, S. M. The Laggan and its people. 1986.
Gunning, Marian. Ancient and forgotten townlands of the Foyle [Strabane: printed by J. D. Print 2000]. Ill. Maps. [Inc descriptions of townlands on both sides of River Foyle].
Porter, Conor. In and Around Raphoe. [Raphoe]: Raphoe Historical Res Group, 1999
About Raphoe – compiled by Raphoe Guild of ICA, 1999.
Mullin, T. H. The Kirk and lands of Convoy since the Scottish Settlement. Belfast Newsletter, 1960.
Historical Notes of Raphoe, Finn Valley, Lifford and Twin Towns.

Mountcharles: see **Donegal Town**

Laghey: Trimble, T. H. The Legacy that is Laghey Community and Church. Letterkenny: printed by Browne (Printers) 2000.

Lettercarn: Lettercarn: An Illustrious Past, and Uncertain Future [s.l.] printed by Seamus de Faoite Print, 1999 [history of Lettercarn area in Templecarn (Pettigo) parish].

Leitirmacaward: Cannon, Karl. A Tour of Lettermacaward, 1985.

Letterkenny: Maguire, Edward. Letterkenny past and present. Letterkenny: McKinney & O'Callaghan [192-]
Fleming, Sam. Letterkenny, past and present [Ballyshannon: printed by Donegal Democrat] [197-]
O'Carroll, Declan. Rockhill House, Letterkenny, Co. Donegal: a history [Ballyshannon: printed by Donegal Democrat] 1984.
Letterkenny Family Roots by Noel Farrell (Longford 1996). Includes listing of: 1901 & 1911 Census; Griffith's Valuation (1858); Slater's Street Directory (1894). (see illustration on next page).

Lough Eske: Devitt, Dermot. A look back at Lough Eske: the western shore: a chronological miscellany [s.l.], Lough Eske Community Development Association, 2004.

Meevagh: Lucas, Leslie. Meevagh down the years. Belfast: Appletree Press, 1983.
Lucas, Leslie. More about Mevagh. Belfast: Appletree Press, 1982.

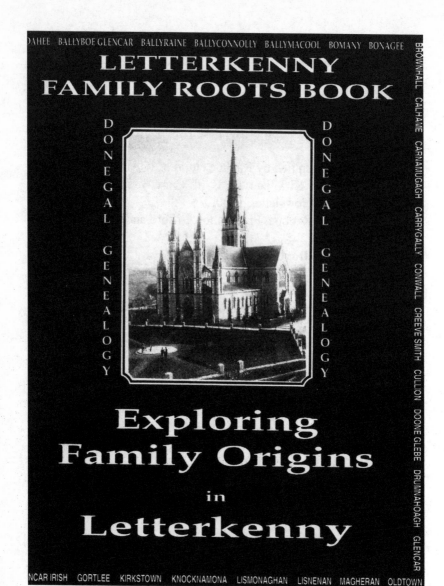

Letterkenny Family Roots by Noel Farrell (Longford 1996).
Includes listing of: 1901 and 1911 Census;
Griffith's Valuation (1858);
Slater's Street Directory (1894)
and a map of Letterkenny (1865).

Milford: Friel, Sheila. Milford towards the Millenium [Milford: Milford Historical Group of the IRD] 1997.

Moville: Montgomery, Henry. A History of Moville and its Neighbourhood. Moville 1991.

Pettigo: O'Gallachair, P. The Parish of Carn [s.l.: s.n., 19-]
O'Connor, D. St Patrick's Purgatory, Lough Derg: It's history traditions, legends, antiquities, topography and scenic surroundings. Dublin: Duffy, 1885.
Cunningham, John B, Lough Derg: legendary pilgrimage. Monaghan 1984.

Ramelton: Tullyaughnish (Ramelton Area) The Parish of Tullyaughnish – Ramelton. Brian Smeaton. Ramelton, Seamus McGee, 1994.

Rathmullan: Parish of Killygarvan. Along Rathmullan's Shore. Margaret Carlton, Mary Bowden, Aine Ní Dhuibhne, Rathmullan, 2001.

Rossnowlagh: Patterson, W. J. Rossnowlagh Remembered [Ballyshannon: printed by Donegal Democrat] 1991.

The Rosses: Ua Cnáimhsí, Padraig. Idir a dá Ghaoth. [B.A.C. Sáirséal Ó Macaigh, 1997.
O'Donnell, Ben. The Story of the Rosses. Edited by John Barry O'Donnell. Lifford: Caorán Press, 1999. 441p. ill.

St. Johnston: Crooks, D. W. T. In the Footsteps of St. Báithín: A History of the Parishes of Taughboyne with Craigadooish, All Saints, Newtowncunningham, Christ Church, Burt and Killie, Carrigans (Ballyshannon: Donegal Democrat) 1993.

Stranorlar: Knights of Columbanus, 1991.
Kelly, David. Rambles round the Finn. Ballyshannon: 1992.

Journals publishing material of interest to Donegal Family History:

Donegal Annual: (Don.Ann) Journal of the Donegal Historical Society
Derriana: Journal of the Derry Diocesan Historical Society.
Clogher Record: Journal of the Clogher Diocesan Historical Society.
Due North: Federation of Ulster Local Studies Journal.

The Spark: Border Counties Books, Clogher, Co. Tyrone – twice yearly.

In addition to these local history periodicals, there are also several periodicals which publish material from all of Ireland, including Donegal.

The Irish Ancestor: (published 1969 to 1986)
The Irish Ancestor was published in 33 issues, plus 4 supplements, containing over 2,500 pages of which some 320 pages included images or photographs. Four supplements were also published, including 'An Index to Raphoe Marriage Licence Bonds, 1710-1755 and 1817-1830' in 1969. This collection of journals is now available on CD-ROM from Eneclann (www.eneclann.ie)

The Irish Genealogist: (published 1937 –)
Includes a huge range of genealogical articles and source material including memorial inscriptions, diocesan wills, family histories etc. The journals from 1937-1993 are available on CD-ROM from Eneclann Publications

Familia: (published 1985 -)
This publication specialises in material of Ulster interest. It is published by the Ulster Historical Foundation, Balmoral Buildings, 12 College Square East, Belfast BT1 6DD which was established in 1956 to promote knowledge of, and interest in, Irish history and genealogy, with particular reference to Ulster. It also publishes the Directory of Irish Family History Research (Subscribers Interest Lists).

North Irish Roots (1984 -)
This periodical is published twice yearly by the North of Ireland Family History Society which is based at Society of Education, 69-71 University Street, Belfast BT7 1HL. It contains materials of relevance to all Ulster counties.

Chapter 16 Useful Addresses

It is useful to note that Donegal material is available in the repositories of two different administrations. Official documents are more likely to be found in Dublin repositories as the county is part of the Republic of Ireland. However, it is physically closer to Belfast and the neighbouring counties of Derry and Fermanagh are part of Northern Ireland. Older material, and material which also deals with the latter counties may therefore be found in Belfast repositories. However, the Dublin and Belfast archives usually have copies of the major sources.

A. National Repositories:

The National Archives of Ireland (NAI)
Bishop Street, Dublin 8
Telephone: 01 407 2333
Email: mail@nationalarchives.ie
Website: www.
nationalarchives.ie

Holdings include 1901 and 1911 census returns, wills and administrations, Griffiths valuations, tithe applotments and official papers. It holds papers of several older repositories including the Public Record Office and the State Paper Office.

Land Commission
Bishop Street, Dublin 8
(same building as National Archives)

Holdings include details of land sales with landowners and tenant rental lists.

National Library of Ireland (NLI)
Kildare Street
Dublin 2
Telephone: 01 603 0200; Fax: 01 676 6690
Email: info@nli.ie
Website: www.nli.ie

RC Church records, Griffiths valuations, tithe applotments, newspapers, Land Commission index, directories and other publications, i.e. journals, etc.

Genealogical Office (GO)
2 Kildare Street
Dublin 2
Telephone: 01 603 0200; Fax:
01 676 6690
Email: info@nli.ie
Website: www.nli.ie

Part of NLI; Extensive collection
of genealogical manuscripts and
family histories.

Registry of Deeds
Henrietta Street, Dublin 1
Telephone: (01) 873 2233
Website: www.irlgov.ie

Deeds registered from 1708,
Grantors index, land indexes,
memorials and abstracts. Entry
fee charged.

Land Registry
(Western Region)
Setanta Centre, Dublin 2

Registration of land title since 1892,
with relevant maps.

Valuation Office
Irish Life Centre, Dublin 1
Telephone: (01) 670 7500; Fax:
(01) 804 8406
Email: davd.hickey@
landregistry.ie
Website: www.irlgove.ie/
landreg

Valuation records (Griffiths and
after), and maps.

Royal Irish Academy (RIA)
19 Dawson Street, Dublin 2
Telephone: (01) 676 2570
Email: library@ria.ie
Website: www.ria.ie

A large collection of manuscripts
and publications.

Trinity College Library (TCD)
College Green, Dublin 2
Telephone: (01) 698 1189; Fax:
(01) 671 9003
Email: mscripts: tcd.ie
Website: www.tcd.ie/Library

A large collection of manuscripts
and publications and Congested
District Board Reports.

General Register Office
Government Offices
Convent Road, Roscommon
Telephone: 090 663 2900; Fax:
(090) 6632999
and
GRO Research Facility
3rd Floor,
Block 7,
Irish Life Centre,
Lower Abbey Street,
Dublin 1
www.groireland.ie

Register of all births, deaths and
marriages in Ireland since 1864.
Church of Ireland marriages since
1845. Fees charged for search and
certificates.

**The Representative Church
Body Library (RCB)**
Braemor Park, Churchtown,
Dublin 14
Telephone: (01) 492 3979
Website: www.ireland.anglican.org/

This library is the chief reference
library of the Church of Ireland.
It holds parish registers as well
as vestry books, preachers' books
and account books. It also has
an extensive collection of
biographical information on C of I
clergymen. An account of records
by RCBL libarian, Dr. Raymond
Refausse is in Chapter 3 of Irish
Church Records (Flyleaf Press,
2001) (see p. 38)

**Presbyterian Historical
Society of Ireland**
Church House, Fisherwick
Place,
Belfast BT1 6DW
Northern Ireland
Website: www.
presbyterianireland.org

Records relating to some
presbyteries and congregations;
baptismal and marriage records
of many congregations; files
detailing records held by
congregations. Files on ministers
of the Presbyterian Church in
Ireland from 1613. Writings by
Presbyterian ministers. Copies.
by Tenison Groves, of census
records.

Methodist Historical Society
Aldersgate House
13 University Road, Belfast
Telephone: 048 795 762

Microfilm of Methodist registers of Northern Ireland circuits. Part of Donegal is in the Enniskillen circuit. Miscellaneous: writings of Methodists: (correspondence, diaries, scrapbooks), photographs and other illustrative material, late 18th-20th century.

Church of Jesus Christ of Latter Day Saints Family History Centre
The Willows
Glasnevin, Dublin 11
Telephone: (01) 830 9960
Website: www.familysearch.org
Also

Holds GRO indexes (microfilm) and certificates for various years; miscellaneous genealogical records.

Family History Centre
401 Hollywood Road
Belfast
Website: www.familysearch.org

Holds similar genealogical material to the Dublin centre.

Department of Folklore University College Dublin (UCD)
Belfield, Dublin 4
Telephone: (01) 693 3244

Has interesting collections of documents and tapes relating to folklore and customs in Donegal.

Public Record Office of Northern Ireland
(PRONI) 66 Balmoral Avenue
Belfast BT9 6NY
Northern Ireland
Telephone: (028) 9025 1318;
Fax: (028) 9025 5999
Email: proni@dcalni.gov.uk
Website: www.proni.gov.uk

Holds genealogical material relating to Donegal in its Landed Estates and Business Records, Solicitors Records, Copies of Church records including parish Registers. Ordnance Survey Maps, 1830-1970, tithe applotment books, 1823-38 and signatories of 1912 Covenant.

B. Local Repositories and Organisations:

Donegal Ancestry Ltd. (DAL)
Old Meeting House
Back Lane
Ramelton, Co. Donegal
Telephone: 074 9151266
Website: www.indigo.ie/
~donances

Holds a substantial amount of Donegal parish registers and other genealogical material. They will conduct research on a fee basis.

Donegal County Library (DCL)
Telephone/Fax: 074 9124950;
E-Mail: central@
donegallibrary.ie
Online Catalogue: www.
donegallibrary.ie

Local history collection, includes 1901 and 1911 Census and other genealogical material.

Donegal County Archives (DCA)
Three Rivers Centre
Lifford, Co. Donegal
Telephone: +353 74 91
72490/455
Fax: +353 74 91 42290
Email: archivist@donegalcoco.ie
Website: www.donegalcoco.ie

Holds records of the Poor Law Unions, Workhouses, Local Government Board, Rural District Councils, Board of Health, Grand Jury, County and other Local Authorities School records and some estate papers, etc. from private sources. See p. 134 for a list of materials

Donegal Historical Society
Secretary: Una McGarrigle
Parkhill, Ballyshannon, Co.
Donegal
Telephone: 071 9851726
Emal: unamcgarrigle@hotmail.
com

Publishes the periodical 'Donegal Annual'

O'Dochartaigh Research Centre
Inch Island, Co. Donegal
Website: www.odochartaigh.
com

A user friendly family run genealogical centre specialising in Co. Donegal family records. Research fee required.

Genealogy Centre Heritage Library
14 Bishop Street
Derry, Co. Derry

Co. Derry archive also contains material on Inishowen parishes, Co. Donegal. Research Fee.

Centre for Migration Studies
Ulster American Folk Park
Mellon Road, Castletown,
Omagh, Co. Tyrone.
BT78 5QY
Telephone: 028 8225 6315
Fax: 028 8224 2241
Email: centremigstudies@ni-libraries.net
Websites: www.qub.ac.uk/cms and
www.folkpark.com

The Research Library at the Centre for Migration Studies comprises a specialist collection of printed material and an Irish Emigration Database. The Irish Emigration Database is a computerised collection of primary source documents on Irish emigration to North America (USA and Canada) in the 18th and 19th centuries.

COUNTY OFFICERS.

Clerk of the Crown, J. Joyce, esq., Strabane.
Clerk of the Peace, James Cochran, esq., Crohan House, Lifford.
Deputy Clerk of the Peace, Mr. John Walwood, Stranorlar.
Sessional Crown Solicitor, Wm. Barrett, esq. Riverstown, Ardara.
Treasurer, Francis Mansfield, esq., Castleshanahan, Letterkenny.
Secretary to Grand Jury, S. Sproule, esq., Rathmelton.
County Surveyor, John Stedman, esq., Letterkenny.
Sub-Sheriff, Samuel J. Crookshank, esq., Derry.
Returning Officer, Robert Crookshank, esq., 3, Henrietta-street, Dublin.
Coroner, # # #
Inspector of Weights and Measures, J. Harvey Goory.
Agents for Lloyds, Mr. J. M'Gloin, Ballyshannon; Mr. A. Cassidy, Killybegs; and Mr. R. Coane, Dunfanaghy.

STAMP DISTRIBUTERS.

Head Distributer for the county, Ralph Young, esq., Letterkenny.
Ballybofey, Mrs. King.
Ballyshannon, John Scott.
Donegal, James Mulraney.
Fahan, Mrs. M'Clelland.
Moville, Patrick M'Kinney.
Pettigoe, H. Hamilton.
Ramelton, Jane Hunter.
Raphoe, Samuel Kerr.

BARONY CESS COLLECTORS.

Banagh, I. O'Donnell, Summy, Ardara.
Boylagh, I. O'Donnell, Summy, Ardara.
Inishowen east, R. Mitchell, Dunross, Moville.
Inishowen west, J. Dysart, Carnamady, Derry.
Kilmacrenan, William Black, Church-hill.
Raphoe, R. Mansfield, Killygordon.
Tyrhugh, J. Hamilton, Rushbrook, Ballintra.

MILITIA STAFF.

Colonel, Right Hon. the Earl of Leitrim.

Dunfanaghy, M. N. Wright.
Glenties, John C. Rodden.
Ramelton, W. Meredith.
Raphoe, A. W. Stafford.

COAST GUARD STATIONS.

Buncrana; Crowris; Dowran; Dunnaff Head; Ennisboffin; Glengad; Guidore; Inniscoo; Loughroris; Malinmore; Mulroy; Port Kenigo; Port Redford; Portnoe; Port Roshin; Rathmullen; Rutland; St. John's point; Sheephaven; Slievebane; Teelin East; Tryhane.

MANOR COURTS.

Ballyshannon; Buncrana, Elagh, Green-castle, and Malm; Castlefin; Castle Boyle and Portin Island; Donegal; Kilmacrenan; Killybegs; Magavlin and Lismeghry; Mughrymore; Orwell and Burleigh; Rathmullen; Stranorlar; Termonmagrath; Tyrhugh.

PETTY SESSIONS COURTS.

Place where held, Day, and Name of Clerk.

Ardara, second Tuesday every month; E. Brice.
Ballintra, second Tuesday; A. Jennings.
Ballyshannon, second Wednesday; W. Curry.
Buncrana, second Thursday; C. O'Donnell.
Burnfoot, Churchtown, third Friday every month; H. G. Cairns.
Church-hill, second Tuesday; R. Pearson.
Carndonagh, third Wednesday; G. H. Hewston.
Cotteen, Dunfanaghy, third Friday; M. Trimency.
Donegal, last Wednesday; J. W. M'Dermott.
Dunfanaghy, second Tuesday; D. M'Kelvey.
Dungloe, third Thursday; W. Hanlon.
Glenties, first Monday; D. M'Devitt.
Killybegs, second Monday; J. Crawford.
Letterkenny, second Wednesday; H. E. Peoples.
Malin, first Wednesday; H. W. Hewston.
Milford, second Thursday; B. D. Heuston.
Moville, first Tuesday; John M'Devitt.
Newtown Cunningham, first Friday; G. W. Kearns.
Pettigo, last Friday; R. P. Edwards.
Ramelton, second Tuesday; G. Doherty.

Typical information that can be found in Thom's Directories (see P. 81)

Index